THE TORONTO

EXPLORER'S BUCKET LIST

Your Ultimate Travel Guide to Toronto's Top Attractions

Brinn Palmer

Disclaimer:

The information provided in **"Toronto Explorer's Bucket List: *Your Ultimate Travel Guide to Toronto's Top Attractions"*** is intended for general informational purposes only. While we strive to ensure the accuracy and reliability of the details within this guide, we cannot guarantee that all information is complete or up-to-date.

We strongly recommend that readers independently verify all details, including hours of operation, admission fees, transportation options, and the availability of attractions and accommodations before making any travel plans.

The inclusion of specific destinations, attractions, accommodations, or services in this guide does not imply endorsement or recommendation by the publisher. Travelers should exercise their own judgment and discretion when exploring Toronto and take necessary precautions for their safety and well-being.

The publisher disclaims any liability for any loss, injury, or inconvenience that may occur as a result of using the information presented in this guide. Travel with awareness, and enjoy discovering all that Toronto has to offer.

How to Use This Guide

This guide is your companion to exploring top attractions and hidden gems. Here's how to make the most of it:

- Browse by Destination: Explore different regions with top attractions and activities listed for each area.
- Plan Your Itinerary: Use detailed descriptions and tips to create a personalized travel plan.
- Check Practical Information: Review key details like hours of operation, fees, and transportation options before heading out.
- Personalize Your Adventure: Adapt the recommendations to fit your travel style and pace.
- Stay Updated: Double-check details like event dates or seasonal changes for the latest information.

Instruction For Using The Interactive QR Code Map

1. Open a QR code scanner app on your smartphone.
2. Allow the app to access your device's camera.
3. Position the QR code within the camera's viewfinder.
4. Scan the QR code by holding your device steady until it's detected.
5. After scanning, you will be linked to Google Maps, directing you to the exact location associated with the QR code.

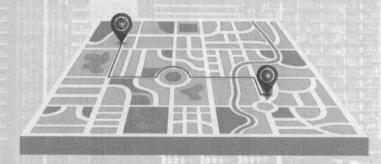

TABLE OF CONTENTS

Welcome to "Toronto Explorer's Bucket List"

Get ready to uncover the best of Toronto with our comprehensive guide to the city's top attractions. Toronto, a bustling metropolis known for its rich cultural fabric and dynamic energy, offers a wide range of experiences that cater to every interest. Our "Toronto Explorer's Bucket List" is designed to help you navigate the must-see landmarks and hidden gems that define this vibrant city.

Start your journey with iconic sites such as the CN Tower, where you can take in panoramic views of the city from one of the tallest freestanding structures in the world. Visit the Royal Ontario Museum to explore its extensive collection of art, natural history, and world cultures, or stroll through the historic Distillery District, renowned for its well-preserved Victorian-era buildings and thriving arts scene.

Kensington Market awaits with its eclectic mix of shops, cafes, and food stalls, offering a taste of Toronto's multicultural flavor. For those seeking outdoor adventures, the Toronto Islands provide a serene escape with beautiful views of the skyline, while High Park offers a large green space perfect for hiking, picnicking, and enjoying seasonal events.

This guide includes practical information on each attraction, such as locations, opening hours, and tips for making the most of your visit. Whether you're exploring Toronto for the first time or returning to rediscover the city, our "Toronto Explorer's Bucket List" will help you plan an exciting and memorable trip. Prepare to experience the best of what Toronto has to offer and create lasting memories along the way. Your adventure in this dynamic city begins now!

A Brief History of Toronto

Toronto, Canada's largest city, has a rich and complex history that stretches back thousands of years. Originally known as the site of the Haudenosaunee and Anishinaabe peoples, the area has been a center of indigenous culture long before European explorers arrived.

Early Indigenous Presence

The land where Toronto now stands was inhabited by various indigenous groups, including the Huron-Wendat, the Haudenosaunee (Iroquois), and the Anishinaabe (Ojibwa). These communities lived in the region for centuries, developing a sophisticated culture and deep connection to the land. They established trade routes and had a rich tradition of storytelling, agriculture, and governance.

European Exploration and Settlement

In the early 17th century, French explorer Samuel de Champlain was one of the first Europeans to visit the area. He was attracted by the strategic location of the natural harbor on Lake Ontario. The French established a fur trading post at the site in 1720, known as Fort Rouillé, which was the precursor to future European settlements.

However, it wasn't until the British took control in the late 18th century that Toronto began to take shape as a city. The British established a settlement known as York in 1793, named in honor of the Duke of York. This settlement was chosen for its defensible position and proximity to the key fur trading routes. York was initially intended to serve as the capital of Upper Canada (now Ontario) and played a significant role during the War of 1812, particularly in the Battle of York in 1813, which saw the American forces capture and then burn much of the town.

Growth and Development

Following the war, York was rebuilt and began to develop rapidly. In 1834, the city was renamed Toronto, a name derived from the Mohawk word "tkaronto," which means "where there are trees standing in the water." This name was chosen to reflect the city's indigenous heritage.

During the 19th century, Toronto saw substantial growth and modernization. The arrival of the railway in the mid-19th century connected Toronto with other major cities and spurred economic development. The city expanded with the construction of significant infrastructure, including public buildings and transportation networks. It also saw an influx of immigrants from Europe, which contributed to its diverse population.

20th Century to Present

Toronto continued to grow throughout the 20th century, evolving from a provincial capital to a major international city. The post-World War II era marked a period of rapid expansion and urban development. The city embraced its role as a global financial hub and became known for its multiculturalism, which is reflected in its vibrant neighborhoods and diverse communities.

In recent decades, Toronto has solidified its position as a leading economic and cultural center. It is known for its impressive skyline, including landmarks like the CN Tower and the Royal Ontario Museum. The city has also become a center for arts and entertainment, with a thriving cultural scene that includes theater, music, and film.

Toronto's history is a reflection of its resilience and adaptability. From its indigenous roots to its current status as a global metropolis, the city's past continues to shape its present and future. Today, Toronto stands as a dynamic and multicultural city, embodying the rich tapestry of its history and the ongoing evolution of its identity.

WHY CHOOSE TORONTO FOR YOUR VACATION?

Toronto is an excellent destination for a vacation due to its vibrant blend of culture, attractions, and experiences. Here's why Toronto should be on your travel radar:

1. Diverse Attractions

Toronto offers a wide range of attractions to suit various interests. Iconic landmarks such as the CN Tower provide breathtaking views of the city, while the Royal Ontario Museum and Art Gallery of Ontario showcase impressive collections of art and artifacts. For those interested in history, the historic Distillery District and Casa Loma offer a glimpse into the city's past.

2. Multicultural Experience

Toronto is known for its multicultural atmosphere. The city's diverse neighborhoods, such as Chinatown, Little Italy, and Kensington Market, offer unique cultural experiences and culinary delights from around the world. Exploring these areas provides a taste of global cultures without leaving the city.

3. Culinary Delights

The city's food scene is as varied as its culture. Toronto boasts a wide range of dining options, from street food and food markets to upscale restaurants. Whether you're craving international cuisine, local specialties, or innovative dishes, Toronto's dining scene has something for every palate.

4. Outdoor Adventures

For nature lovers, Toronto offers beautiful parks and outdoor spaces. High Park, with its hiking trails and cherry blossoms, provides a peaceful retreat. The Toronto Islands, just a short ferry ride away, offer scenic views and recreational activities such as biking and kayaking.

5. Arts and Entertainment

Toronto is a hub for arts and entertainment. The city hosts numerous festivals, concerts, and theater performances throughout the year. The Toronto International Film Festival is a major event that attracts filmmakers and celebrities from around the world. Additionally, the vibrant nightlife scene includes everything from live music and comedy shows to trendy bars and clubs.

6. Shopping and Local Finds

Shopping enthusiasts will find plenty to explore, from high-end boutiques and shopping malls to local markets and unique stores. The Eaton Centre and Yorkville are popular shopping destinations, while St. Lawrence Market offers a range of local and artisanal products.

7. Accessibility and Connectivity

Toronto is well-connected, with an efficient public transit system, including buses, streetcars, and the subway, making it easy to get around the city. The city's layout and infrastructure are designed to accommodate tourists, ensuring a smooth and enjoyable visit.

8. Family-Friendly Activities

Toronto is a great destination for families. The city features attractions like the Toronto Zoo, Ripley's Aquarium, and the Ontario Science Centre, which are engaging for children and educational for all ages.

BEST TIME TO VISIT TORONTO FOR VACATION

Toronto is a year-round destination with each season offering its own unique charm. However, the best time to visit largely depends on your interests and what you want to experience. Here's a breakdown of what you can expect throughout the year:

1. Spring (March to May)

Spring in Toronto is a lovely time to visit as the city starts to warm up and the parks and gardens begin to bloom. Temperatures range from cool to mild, making it comfortable for exploring. This is also the season when the cherry blossoms in High Park are in full bloom, creating picturesque views. Spring is a great time for outdoor activities and avoiding the summer tourist crowds.

2. Summer (June to August)

Summer is the peak tourist season in Toronto, characterized by warm weather and a bustling city atmosphere. Temperatures can range from the mid-70s to the low 80s Fahrenheit (20s to 30s Celsius). This is an excellent time to enjoy outdoor festivals, street fairs, and attractions like the Toronto Islands and outdoor patios. The city's vibrant festivals, including the Toronto International Film Festival and Caribana, take place during this season.

3. Fall (September to November)

Fall is another wonderful time to visit Toronto. The weather is generally mild and comfortable, with temperatures ranging from the 50s to 60s Fahrenheit (10s to 20s Celsius). The fall foliage in Toronto's parks and neighborhoods provides stunning views. Fall also marks the beginning of the cultural season, with numerous events, concerts, and theater productions. It's a good time to explore the city without the summer crowds.

4. Winter (December to February)

Winter in Toronto can be cold, with temperatures often dropping below freezing and occasional snowfall. However, the city transforms into a winter wonderland with festive lights and holiday markets. If you enjoy winter activities, you can explore ice skating rinks, winter festivals, and cozy indoor attractions. The city's winter season is less crowded, making it easier to visit popular sites without long lines.

Ultimately, the best time to visit Toronto depends on your personal preferences and what you want to do while you're there.

MUSEUMS AND ART GALLERIES

Royal Ontario Museum
Location: 100 Queens Park, Toronto, ON M5S 2C6, Canada
Plus Code: MJ94+33 Toronto, Ontario, Canada
Contact: +1 416-586-8000
Website: www.rom.on.ca
Opening Hours:
Monday to Sunday: 10 am – 5:30 pm
Description: The Royal Ontario Museum is one of the largest museums in North America, renowned for its extensive collection that spans across history, art, and natural science. The museum houses over six million objects, showcasing diverse cultures and natural wonders from around the globe. Visitors are encouraged to explore the fascinating exhibits of ancient Greek and Korean artifacts, including sculptures, pottery, textiles, and ceremonial items. The museum's expansive galleries include popular sections on dinosaurs, ancient civilizations, and animal life. There are also rotating exhibitions with specialized themes, which may have an additional fee. Families will find the children's area especially engaging, offering creative play and educational activities. It's highly recommended that you purchase tickets in advance to ensure timely access. If you're planning multiple visits, consider opting for a membership, which provides free entrance to exhibitions and other perks. The museum features a café and a restaurant where you can take breaks, as well as a play area for children. Plan your visit early in the day to fully enjoy the extensive collection without rushing.
Nearby Attractions: The Royal Ontario Museum is located near Queen's Park and the University of Toronto, which are also popular attractions for visitors. Additionally, the Bata Shoe Museum and Gardiner Museum, both offering unique collections, are within walking distance.
Important Information for Visitors: Tickets can be purchased online, and it is recommended to book in advance, especially on weekends. Membership options offer great value if you plan multiple visits. The museum provides a variety of kid-friendly activities and has an accessible layout for visitors of all ages.

Art Gallery of Ontario
Location: 317 Dundas St W, Toronto, ON M5T 1G4, Canada
Plus Code: MJ34+CX Toronto, Ontario, Canada
Contact: +1 416-979-6648
Website: www.ago.ca

Opening Hours:
Monday: Closed
Tuesday: 10:30 am – 5 pm
Wednesday: 10:30 am – 9 pm
Thursday: 10:30 am – 5 pm
Friday: 10:30 am – 9 pm
Saturday: 10:30 am – 5:30 pm
Sunday: 10:30 am – 5:30 pm

Description: The Art Gallery of Ontario (AGO) is a premier cultural destination in Toronto, housing an impressive collection of over 90,000 works from different periods, including European masterpieces, contemporary art, and notable Canadian collections. Visitors can explore the expansive galleries, which cover five floors, featuring everything from 10th-century religious carvings to cutting-edge modern art. Special exhibitions are frequently held, and admission often includes these exhibits at no additional cost. The building itself is an architectural marvel, offering an inspiring setting to reflect on art. For families, children enjoy free admission, making it a highly affordable cultural experience. With on-site amenities like the AGO Bistro, a café, a gift shop, and accessible facilities, the gallery ensures a comfortable visit for all guests. There's a checkroom available for a small fee. It's recommended to arrive early in the day to fully enjoy the extensive exhibits, and memberships are available for frequent visitors. The AGO also hosts classes and workshops, enhancing the visitor experience with opportunities for deeper engagement with the arts.

Nearby Attractions: Located in the heart of downtown Toronto, the AGO is close to other major attractions such as the Ontario College of Art and Design (OCAD), Grange Park, and the University of Toronto. The nearby Kensington Market and Chinatown are vibrant neighborhoods worth exploring for food, shopping, and culture.

Important Information for Visitors: Free admission for children makes it an excellent family destination. It is advisable to book tickets in advance for special exhibitions, as they can be popular. Wheelchair access is available, but signage for elevators and restrooms can be unclear, so ask staff for assistance when needed.

Textile Museum of Canada
Location: 55 Centre Ave, Toronto, ON M5G 2H5, Canada
Plus Code: MJ37+R8 Toronto, Ontario, Canada
Contact: +1 416-599-5321
Website: www.textilemuseum.ca

Opening Hours:
Monday: Closed
Tuesday to Saturday: 12 pm – 5 pm
Wednesday: 12 pm – 6 pm
Sunday: Closed

Description: The Textile Museum of Canada offers a unique cultural experience, showcasing an impressive variety of textiles from around the world. Exhibitions explore everything from indigenous Canadian woven clothing to textiles from historic moments like the Underground Railroad. Visitors can engage with hands-on activities, such as weaving and sewing, under the guidance of the museum's staff. The museum, though small, presents a rich collection across two levels, with exhibits rotating regularly. Its intimate setting allows for a thorough visit in about 45 to 90 minutes, making it a convenient stop for those interested in art, history, and culture. Admission is $19 for adults, with options for free passes available through local libraries. The museum also features a shop offering textiles and goods from various regions, adding to the immersive experience. Parking is available at affordable rates right in front of the museum, and the location is tucked away from the hustle and bustle of downtown Toronto, providing a quiet and reflective atmosphere.

Nearby Attractions: Located in downtown Toronto, the museum is close to Nathan Phillips Square and the Art Gallery of Ontario. The nearby quiet streets are perfect for a leisurely stroll after your visit.

Important Information for Visitors: For hands-on activities, be sure to ask about the museum's workshops, where you can participate in weaving and sewing sessions. Also, check for any special fundraising sales during your visit, which may allow free admission.

Niagara Falls

Location: 5705 Falls Avenue, Niagara Falls, Ontario, Canada L2H 6T3

Plus Code: 7H2M+PQ Niagara Falls, Ontario, Canada

Contact: 905-356-7625

Website: www.niagarafalls.ca

Opening Hours: Open daily; hours vary by season. The Maid of the Mist boat tour operates from April to November.

Description: Niagara Falls is a breathtaking natural wonder located on the border between Ontario, Canada, and New York, USA. It consists of three magnificent waterfalls: the Horseshoe Falls on the Canadian side, and the Bridal Veil and American Falls on the New York side. The Horseshoe Falls, the largest of the three, offers a stunning view from the Canadian side. Visitors can take advantage of various attractions including the Skylon Tower, which provides panoramic views of the falls from its observation deck, and the Maid of the Mist boat tour, which offers a close-up experience of the powerful cascades. For a more immersive experience, elevators take visitors to a lower viewpoint behind the falls, where the force of the water can be felt up close. The surrounding area features numerous viewing platforms, hiking trails, and boardwalks, allowing visitors to enjoy the falls from different perspectives. The site also includes modern amenities such as a gift shop, cafes, and restrooms.

Nearby Attractions: The American Falls and Bridal Veil Falls on the U.S. side, and various parks and observation points like Goat Island and Luna Island.

Important Information for Visitors: Parking is available for $10.00 per day. It is highly recommended to wear waterproof clothing as the mist from the falls can soak visitors even on dry days. The area can get crowded, especially during peak tourist seasons, so arriving early can enhance the experience. The gift shop offers a wide range of souvenirs, though prices may be high.

Toronto Police Museum and Discovery Centre
Location: 40 College St, Toronto, ON M5G 2J3, Canada
Plus Code: MJ68+F3 Toronto, Ontario, Canada
Contact: +1 416-808-7020
Website: www.tps.ca
Opening Hours:
Monday to Friday: 8:30 am – 4 pm
Saturday: Closed
Sunday: Closed

Description: The Toronto Police Museum and Discovery Centre, located inside the Toronto Police Headquarters, offers a fascinating glimpse into the history and evolution of the Toronto Police Service. This free-to-enter museum showcases a wide variety of memorabilia, including vintage police uniforms, badges, motorcycles, and vehicles. The exhibits also cover important historical events and honor fallen officers who lost their lives in the line of duty. Interactive displays, such as a ride-on police motorcycle, enhance the visitor experience and are particularly popular with children. Although small, the museum packs a lot into its space, offering a deeper understanding of law enforcement's role in Toronto's development. Visitors can also stop by the on-site gift shop for unique Toronto Police merchandise.
A quick security check is required upon entering the building, and the museum is wheelchair accessible. While some exhibits could use updates, and funding is limited, the museum provides an engaging and informative experience for those interested in policing and history. Reservations are not required for individual visits.
Nearby Attractions: The museum is located near Toronto's Discovery District and is within walking distance of College Park and the University

of Toronto's St. George campus. The area offers a variety of dining and shopping options.

Important Information for Visitors: The museum is free to enter, making it a cost-effective destination for families and law enforcement enthusiasts. Be aware that the gift shop may close earlier than the museum itself, so plan accordingly if you wish to purchase items.

Hockey Hall of Fame
Location: 30 Yonge St, Toronto, ON M5E 1X8, Canada
(Located on Floor 1 of Brookfield Place)
Plus Code: JJWC+WW Toronto, Ontario, Canada
Contact: +1 416-360-7735
Website: www.hhof.com

Opening Hours:
Monday to Sunday: 10:00 am – 6:00 pm

Description: The Hockey Hall of Fame is an iconic destination for hockey fans and those curious about the sport's rich history. Located in the heart of downtown Toronto, this museum showcases a vast collection of hockey memorabilia, including famous trophies like the original and traveling versions of the Stanley Cup. The Hall features interactive exhibits, including a chance to play goalie or shooter in simulated hockey games, making it a fantastic destination for both kids and adults.

The museum houses exhibits on the NHL, international hockey, Olympic teams, and various hockey dynasties throughout the years. One of the highlights is the Great Hall, which displays all the trophies, including the Stanley Cup, updated with the latest engravings from the current season. Visitors can also explore displays of hockey jerseys from around the world and enjoy an immersive 3D show produced by TSN.

Don't miss the replica of the Canadiens locker room and the "Mask" section showcasing the evolution of goalie masks. There is also a gift shop offering hockey-related merchandise, and for an extra fee, visitors can take an official photo with Lord Stanley's Cup.

Visitor Tips:
- Great for families with kids thanks to interactive exhibits.

- No need to book in advance for individual visits, and the museum rarely has a long wait time.
- Consider visiting on a weekday when it's less crowded.
- Allocate a few hours to explore, as there is plenty to see and do.
- Touching and hugging the Stanley Cup is allowed!

Nearby Attractions: The Hockey Hall of Fame is located in Brookfield Place, within walking distance of the Toronto waterfront, Union Station, and several dining and shopping options.

TRAVEL

DATE:

DURATION:

DESTINATION:

PLACES TO SEE:

1 _____
2 _____
3 _____
4 _____
5 _____
6 _____
7 _____

LOCAL FOOD TO TRY:

1 _____
2 _____
3 _____
4 _____
5 _____
6 _____
7 _____

NOTES

EXPENSES IN TOTAL:

JOURNAL

- Consider visiting in the summer or autumn when the surrounding gardens are in full bloom and the trails in Thomson Memorial Park are beautiful for a leisurely stroll.
- Check for any ongoing events or special activities as they can enhance the experience, especially for families.

Nearby Attractions: Thomson Memorial Park is located around the museum, offering walking trails, picnic areas, a dog park, and lots of outdoor activities. It's a peaceful escape within the city.

Mackenzie House
Location: 82 Bond St, Toronto, ON M5B 1X2, Canada
Plus Code: MJ4C+7J Toronto, Ontario, Canada
Contact: +1 416-392-6915
Website: www.toronto.ca

Opening Hours:
Wednesday to Sunday: 11:00 am – 5:00 pm
Monday and Tuesday: Closed
Description:
Mackenzie House is a historic site and museum located in downtown Toronto, offering visitors a fascinating look at the life and times of William Lyon Mackenzie, Toronto's first mayor and a key leader of the 1837 Upper Canada Rebellion. The house was Mackenzie's final home before his death in 1861. This 19th-century Georgian townhouse has been preserved and restored to reflect the period during which Mackenzie lived there.
Visitors can explore the home's original furnishings, artifacts, and a fully operational 19th-century print shop that Mackenzie used for his publications. Tours offer in-depth insights into Mackenzie's tumultuous life, the rebellion, and his role in shaping early Canadian politics. The staff and tour guides are knowledgeable, and they engage guests with interactive experiences, such as printing your own newspapers or creating bookmarks.
Mackenzie House frequently offers special workshops, historical presentations, and events, making it a fun and educational destination for families, history buffs, and curious visitors alike. Admission is free, adding to its appeal as a must-see historical attraction in Toronto.

Visitor Tips:

- Admission is free for all visitors.
- Interactive experiences, such as printing workshops, are available, providing hands-on learning opportunities.
- Plan for about an hour to explore the house and participate in activities.
- The museum often holds events and workshops, so checking the schedule in advance is recommended.

Nearby Attractions: Mackenzie House is located in the heart of downtown Toronto, so visitors can easily access other cultural and historical attractions, as well as nearby shops and restaurants.

Aga Khan Museum
Location: 77 Wynford Dr, North York, ON M3C 1K1, Canada
Plus Code: PMG9+44 North York, Ontario, Canada
Contact: +1 416-646-4677
Website: agakhanmuseum.org
Opening Hours:

- Monday: Closed
- Tuesday to Sunday: 10:00 am – 5:30 pm
- Wednesday: Extended hours until 8:00 pm

Description:

The Aga Khan Museum is an exceptional cultural institution dedicated to presenting Islamic art, heritage, and culture. Located in North York, Toronto, the museum showcases a rich collection of historical artifacts, artworks, and exhibitions that offer insights into the Islamic world's artistic, intellectual, and cultural contributions. The museum's architecture itself is a stunning minimalist design, creating a serene atmosphere that complements the exhibits within.

Permanent exhibitions display a variety of Islamic artifacts, from manuscripts and calligraphy to ancient architectural pieces. The museum also features rotating temporary exhibitions such as the immersive "Light: Visionary Perspectives" exhibit, which explores the symbolism and impact of light in art and culture. Visitors will appreciate the thoughtful curation, which spans several centuries and regions, offering a broad yet in-depth view of Islamic art and history.

The Aga Khan Museum offers guided tours, interactive workshops, and special events, making it an engaging destination for visitors of all ages. The museum grounds are beautifully maintained, offering tranquil outdoor spaces with water features and gardens, enhancing the overall visitor experience.

Facilities:
- **Café:** Offers a selection of sandwiches and beverages, providing a nice spot to relax after exploring the museum.
- **Gift Shop:** A diverse range of items, though some reviews suggest the service may need improvement.
- **Parking:** Available for a flat fee of $10.
- **Accessibility:** Fully accessible with elevators and spacious layouts.

Visitor Tips:
- **PRESTO Card Discount:** Offers a discounted ticket price for those using public transit.
- **Free Wednesdays:** Extended evening hours provide a relaxed opportunity to explore the museum after regular hours.
- **No Wait:** Visitors typically experience little to no wait time.
- **Special Events:** Keep an eye on the museum's event schedule for workshops, tours, and special exhibitions.

Nearby Attractions: The museum is a short drive away from other attractions in North York and Toronto, making it easy to include in a day of cultural exploration.

Fort York National Historic Site
Location: 250 Fort York Blvd, Toronto, ON M5V 3K9, Canada
Plus Code: JHQW+M8 Toronto, Ontario, Canada
Contact: +1 416-392-6907
Website: toronto.ca
Opening Hours:
- Monday and Tuesday: Closed
- Wednesday to Sunday: 11:00 am – 5:00 pm

Description: Fort York National Historic Site is one of Toronto's largest and most significant historical museums, offering a fascinating glimpse into the city's military history. Fort York played a key role in the War of 1812 and is home to some of Toronto's oldest structures, including barracks, magazines, and fortifications. The site is spread across 43 acres and includes a number of original and restored buildings from the 19th century.

Visitors are invited to explore the barracks, the stone magazine (where gunpowder was stored), and many other preserved areas that depict the lives of soldiers stationed at the fort. The fort also houses an extensive collection of cannons and artillery, providing an immersive military history experience. Daily tours offer visitors a deeper understanding of the site's significance, with guides sharing knowledge about the Battle of York and life at the fort. Additionally, the musket firing demonstrations are a highlight of the visit, showcasing historical weaponry in action.

The new visitor center is another valuable addition to the site, featuring exhibits, multimedia presentations, and archaeological discoveries related to the fort's history. There's also a commemorative room dedicated to the Battle of York.

Facilities:
- **Gift Shop:** Offers a range of historical memorabilia and gifts.
- **Visitor Center:** Features temporary exhibits, educational films, and historical displays.
- **Community Garden:** Located at the northeast end of the site, a lesser-known but lovely feature.

Visitor Tips:
- **Guided Tours:** Available at the top of every hour and highly recommended for enhancing the experience.
- **Demonstrations:** Musket firing demonstrations are a popular attraction and add an exciting layer of historical immersion.
- **Best Time to Visit:** On mild days, as much of the site is outdoors, and there is limited protection from the sun or heat.
- **Accessibility:** Be aware that some areas may require walking across uneven terrain.
- **Admission:** Free admission makes it a cost-effective visit for history enthusiasts.

High Park
Location: 1873 Bloor St W, Toronto, ON M6R 2Z3, Canada
Plus code: JGWP+JG Toronto, Ontario, Canada
Contact: +1 416-338-0338
Website: www.highparktoronto.com
Opening hours: Open 24 hours

Description: High Park is Toronto's largest public park and a prime destination for outdoor enthusiasts and nature lovers. The park features a vast expanse of green spaces, beautiful cherry blossoms in the spring, and a diverse array of recreational activities. Key attractions include a zoo with various animals such as peacocks, highland cattle, and llamas, a large playground with a splash pad, and a trackless train for children. The park also offers ample areas for picnics, dog walking (with designated off-leash zones), and sports facilities. The well-maintained grounds and tranquil ponds make it an ideal spot for relaxation and family outings. Accessible via subway, High Park provides a serene escape from city life. Note that parking can be challenging, especially on weekends, as cars are restricted within the park.

Nearby Attractions: The park's close proximity to the lakefront and the ability to view historical architecture adds to its appeal. Nearby amenities include various eateries and greenhouses.

Important Information for Visitors:

- On weekends, parking is limited, and cars are not allowed inside the park. It is recommended to use public transit or park on the main street.
- Restrooms are available near the playgrounds, pool, and certain eateries.
- A small fee of $7 per adult is charged for the trackless train ride around the park.

Toronto Zoo
Location: 2000 Meadowvale Rd, Toronto, ON M1B 5K7, Canada
Plus code: RR97+4R Toronto, Ontario, Canada
Contact: +1 416-392-5900
Website: www.torontozoo.com

Opening hours: Daily: 9am – 7pm

Description: The Toronto Zoo is a premier wildlife destination featuring an extensive collection of animals from around the world, including tigers, bears, apes, snakes, and fish. The zoo is known for its cleanliness and expansive layout, providing a comprehensive and enjoyable experience for visitors. To explore the entire zoo, plan for about 6 to 8 hours. Highlights include a large splash pad suitable for young children, a train ride for a convenient tour of the grounds, and diverse continent-specific animal exhibits. The zoo also offers ample parking at $15 per visit or $50 for an annual pass. Facilities include a Tim Hortons, various food options, and picnic areas. It is recommended to bring a refillable water bottle and comfortable walking shoes, as extensive walking is required. The zoo is accessible via a zoo mobile, and visitors with a Presto card can receive a 10% discount.

Nearby Attractions: The Toronto Zoo is located within a natural setting that complements the zoo experience. Visitors can also explore nearby parks and recreational areas.

Important Information for Visitors:
- Reservations are recommended.
- Parking is available but limited; arriving early can secure a better spot.
- Large areas of the zoo, including the Canada section, may involve significant walking and hilly terrain.
- Check the zoo's website or contact them for updates on construction or other changes that may affect your visit.

Casa Loma

Location: 1 Austin Terrace, Toronto, ON M5R 1X8, Canada
Plus code: MHHR+66 Toronto, Ontario, Canada
Contact: +1 416-923-1171
Website: www.casaloma.ca
Opening hours: Daily: 9:30am – 5pm
Description: Casa Loma is a historic castle in Toronto, originally built as a private residence and now functioning as a museum. Visitors can explore the expansive mansion, which includes private collections, various artworks, and historical artifacts. The castle's grandeur and historical significance offer a glimpse into the opulent lifestyle of its former owner. Key features include a grand banquet hall, beautifully maintained gardens, and a long tunnel connecting the main house to the garage and stable. Although the site provides a rich historical experience, it may not appeal to all visitors due to its focus on collections and historical context. Accessibility can be challenging, with many areas requiring navigation of steep and narrow stairs, which may be difficult for those with mobility issues. The castle's interior can also be warm, as air conditioning is not uniformly distributed. For those interested in the grandeur of historic homes and detailed exhibitions, Casa Loma offers a captivating experience.

Nearby Attractions: Casa Loma is situated in a historic area with other cultural sites nearby. The castle's elevated location also provides scenic city views.

Important Information for Visitors:
- Parking is available with an attendant, though fees may apply.
- Pre-purchased tickets are recommended to avoid waiting in line.
- The site is not fully accessible for those with mobility issues.
- Comfortable walking shoes are recommended due to extensive stairs and walking areas.

Toronto Music Garden
Location: 479 Queens Quay W, Toronto, ON M5V 3M8, Canada
Plus code: JJP4+Q7 Toronto, Ontario, Canada
Contact: +1 416-973-4000
Website: www.toronto.ca
Opening hours: Daily: Open 24 hours
Description: The Toronto Music Garden is a unique waterfront park designed to reflect the rhythms and movements of Bach's music, specifically his suite for unaccompanied cello. The garden features a beautifully landscaped environment with pathways and plantings arranged to evoke the structure and flow of musical compositions. Visitors can enjoy the serene atmosphere, shaded spots, and scenic views of the harbor and CN Tower. The garden is an excellent location for picnics, leisurely walks, and relaxation. In summer, it often hosts live performances, adding to its vibrant and culturally enriched ambiance. While the garden's compact size and lack of extensive amenities might limit its appeal for some, its innovative design and tranquil setting make it a worthwhile visit.

Nearby Attractions: Located along the waterfront, the garden offers views of Toronto's harborfront and is close to other waterfront attractions.
Important Information for Visitors:
- There is one public restroom available nearby.
- The garden can get crowded, especially during summer, so plan visits accordingly.
- It's a great spot for leisurely strolls, picnics, and enjoying live performances during the warmer months.

Toronto Island Park
Location: Toronto, ON, Canada
Plus code: JJFG+24 Toronto, Ontario, Canada
Contact: +90 531 278 70 46
Website: www.toronto.ca
Opening hours: Daily: 9am – 5pm
Description: Toronto Island Park, a short ferry ride from downtown Toronto, offers a tranquil escape from the city's hustle and bustle. The island provides stunning views of the Toronto skyline and Lake Ontario, making it an ideal spot for outdoor activities such as yachting, tennis, swimming, and volleyball. Visitors can enjoy leisurely strolls, bike rides, or picnics while taking in the scenic beauty. The island is well-maintained with clean facilities, ample picnic areas, and playgrounds for children. For a unique experience, visitors can also catch glimpses of airplanes landing at Billy Bishop Airport. The ferry ride to the island is a highlight in itself, offering a pleasant way to begin your visit. The park is a great choice for a relaxing day trip with family or friends.

Nearby Attractions: Central Island Beach and Hanlan's Point Beach are notable spots on the island for swimming and sunbathing.

Important Information for Visitors:

- Ferry prices: Adult: $9.11, Senior (65+): $5.86, Youth (Under 19): $5.86, Junior (Under 14): $4.28, Infant: Free.
- It is advisable to bring your own food as options on the island can be expensive.
- The park is suitable for picnics, biking, and walking; bikes and cycle rentals are available.
- Restrooms are clean and conveniently located.

Centreville Amusement Park

Location: 9 Queens Quay W, Toronto, ON M5J 2H3, Canada

Plus code: JJCG+4H Toronto, Ontario, Canada

Contact: +1 416-203-0405

Website: www.centreisland.ca

Opening hours:

- Thursday: 10:30am – 7pm
- Friday: 10:30am – 7pm
- Saturday: 10:30am – 8pm
- Sunday: 10:30am – 8pm
- Monday: 10:30am – 7pm
- Tuesday: 10:30am – 7pm
- Wednesday: 10:30am – 7pm

Description: Centreville Amusement Park, located on Centre Island, offers a charming and family-friendly escape just a short ferry ride from downtown Toronto. The park is designed for a relaxed experience with a variety of gentle rides and attractions suitable for children and families. Popular features include the bumper cars, cable car sky-ride, and a quaint zoo. The park also provides opportunities for games and leisurely strolls around the picturesque surroundings by Lake Ontario. Although the park is known for its enjoyable atmosphere, it's recommended to visit on weekdays or during non-peak hours to avoid crowds, especially during weekends and public holidays. While the park's food options are limited and may not cater to all dietary needs, it remains a delightful destination for a fun-filled day out.

Nearby Attractions: The nearby beaches on Centre Island offer additional recreational options.

Important Information for Visitors:

- It is advisable to check ferry schedules and plan your trip accordingly.
- Consider bringing your own food or snacks due to limited dining options.
- The park is LGBTQ+ friendly and offers a relaxed environment for all visitors.

Trillium Park
Location: 955 Lake Shore Blvd W, Toronto, ON M6K 3B9, Canada
Located in: Ontario Place
Plus code: JHJR+23 Toronto, Ontario, Canada
Contact: +1 416-314-9900
Website: ontarioplace.com
Opening hours:

- Thursday: 6am – 11pm
- Friday: 6am – 11pm
- Saturday: 6am – 11pm
- Sunday: 6am – 11pm
- Monday: 6am – 11pm
- Tuesday: 6am – 11pm
- Wednesday: 6am – 11pm

Description: Trillium Park is a scenic green space situated along Toronto's waterfront, offering breathtaking views of the city skyline and Lake Ontario. This 7.5-acre park, formerly a parking lot, has been transformed into a vibrant natural oasis. The park features the William G. Davis Trail, native plants, trees, and unique sedimentary rocks. It's ideal for cycling, walking, running, and picnicking, with plenty of open spaces for relaxation. The park also honors Indigenous heritage with its moccasin-shaped rock garden and fire pit.

Visitors are drawn to Trillium Park for its tranquil ambiance, especially during the evening hours when the skyline and waterfront views become even more captivating. Throughout the summer, the park hosts free concerts, making it an even more delightful experience. Despite ongoing construction due to the redevelopment of Ontario Place, which limits access to some parts of the park and trail, Trillium Park still offers a refreshing escape from city life.

Nearby Attractions: The park is located within Ontario Place, making it close to various entertainment options and the iconic CN Tower.

Important Information for Visitors:

- Restrooms are available near the entrance and are heated and well-maintained.
- The park is dog-friendly, as long as pets are kept on a leash.

- With ongoing construction in parts of Ontario Place, it's advisable to enter the park from the Hotel X side.

Highlights:
- Great for a relaxing walk or jog.
- Beautiful panoramic views of the city.
- Ideal for picnics with plenty of designated areas.
- Hosts evening light festivals and concerts in the summer.

Simcoe Park
Location: 255 Wellington St W, Toronto, ON M5V 3G5, Canada
Plus code: JJV7+W6 Toronto, Ontario, Canada
Contact: +1 416-338-4386
Website: toronto.ca
Opening hours: Open 24 hours
Description: Simcoe Park is a quaint urban green space located in downtown Toronto, close to notable landmarks like the Metro Toronto Convention Centre, the CBC Broadcasting Centre, and the Ritz-Carlton Hotel. This peaceful park is adorned with beautiful sculptures, including a dramatic mountain piece and a somber workers' memorial honoring those who lost their lives on the job. It's a perfect spot to take a break, enjoy lunch, or people-watch amid the city's hustle and bustle.

Situated near the CN Tower, Simcoe Park also provides access to Toronto's underground PATH system, making it convenient for commuters. Visitors can easily access a food court located beneath the park, offering shelter and dining options during rainy weather.

Highlights:
- Sculptures and memorials that enhance the park's aesthetic appeal.
- Ideal for relaxing, enjoying lunch, or people-watching.
- Convenient access to the underground PATH system and a nearby food court.

Restroom information: Restrooms are located in the food court underneath the park, open from 6 am to 9 pm most days.

Harbourfront Centre

Location: 235 Queens Quay W, Toronto, ON M5J 2G8, Canada

Plus code: JJQ9+G6 Toronto, Ontario, Canada

Contact: +1 416-973-4000

Website: harbourfrontcentre.com

Opening hours:

- **Thursday:** 12–6 pm
- **Friday:** 12–6 pm
- **Saturday, Sunday, Monday, Tuesday:** Closed
- **Wednesday:** 12–6 pm

Description: Harbourfront Centre is a dynamic cultural hub located along the scenic waterfront of Toronto, known for hosting a wide range of artistic and cultural events throughout the year. From lively music festivals and art exhibitions to theater performances and literary readings, it is a vibrant destination where visitors can experience the best of local and international talent. The area boasts breathtaking views of Lake Ontario, creating the perfect setting for relaxing strolls along the boardwalk or engaging in outdoor activities like kayaking, sailing, and cycling.

In addition to its rich cultural offerings, Harbourfront Centre also has a variety of dining options ranging from casual cafes to more upscale restaurants. Visitors can enjoy delicious meals while soaking in the stunning waterfront views. The Centre is especially popular in the summer, with numerous festivals, live shows, and concerts—many of which are free.

Highlights:

- Year-round cultural events including festivals, art exhibitions, and performances.
- Scenic waterfront location with panoramic views of Lake Ontario.
- Recreational activities such as kayaking, cycling, and sailing.
- Family-friendly programs, interactive workshops, and activities for children.
- Numerous dining options with a variety of cuisines.

Restroom information: Restrooms are available but can become messy during busy times and need more regular cleaning.

Recommendations: Visit on weekends in the summer for vibrant festivals, good food, and live concerts. Parking can be a challenge, so plan ahead. Consider bringing your bike to explore the area more easily.

Tommy Thompson Park
Location: 1 Leslie St, Toronto, ON M4M 3M2, Canada
Plus code: JMPG+33 Toronto, Ontario, Canada
Contact: +1 416-661-6600
Website: tommythompsonpark.ca
Opening hours:
- **Thursday - Friday:** 4–9 pm
- **Saturday - Sunday:** 5:30 am–9 pm
- **Monday - Wednesday:** 4–9 pm

Description: Tommy Thompson Park, also known as the Leslie Street Spit, is a nature haven situated just minutes from downtown Toronto. It's a prime location for bird watching, hiking, cycling, and fishing. The park features long walking and cycling trails along the lakefront, offering peaceful natural surroundings, diverse wildlife, and impressive views of the Toronto skyline.

Though it's ideal for outdoor activities like walking and birdwatching, the park is not well-suited for picnics due to the lack of shaded areas and seating spots. Visitors are encouraged to bring plenty of water and any food they need as there are no vendors or restaurants in the park. Despite this, it offers stunning opportunities to experience nature, from observing swans and other birds to appreciating the serene waters.

The park is popular with cyclists and provides bike rental options before the main entrance. It is a great place to escape the city's noise and immerse yourself in nature.

Highlights:
- Bird watching, particularly for swans, geese, and ducks.
- Peaceful walking and cycling trails along Lake Ontario.
- Beautiful views of both the lake and the Toronto skyline.
- Natural, quiet atmosphere, great for relaxation.

Restroom information: Restrooms are available but limited. Be sure to plan accordingly.

Recommendations: Bring your own food, drinks, and plenty of water, as there are no food vendors on-site. Weekdays tend to be quieter than weekends, offering a more serene experience. Red ants may be present in the area, so be cautious when choosing spots to rest.

Riverdale Park West
Location: 375 Sumach St, Toronto, ON M4X 1B8, Canada
Plus code: MJ8R+7F Toronto, Ontario, Canada
Contact: +1 416-392-8188
Website: toronto.ca
Opening hours: Open 24 hours

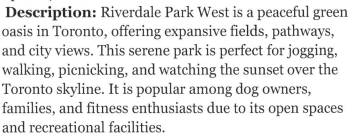

Description: Riverdale Park West is a peaceful green oasis in Toronto, offering expansive fields, pathways, and city views. This serene park is perfect for jogging, walking, picnicking, and watching the sunset over the Toronto skyline. It is popular among dog owners, families, and fitness enthusiasts due to its open spaces and recreational facilities.

The park has a variety of amenities, including picnic tables, benches, a cooling area during summer, and a nearby running track. For kids, there's a playground located at the north end near the swimming pool. Riverdale Park West is also home to Riverdale Farm, a charming spot for kids and adults to visit farm animals.

Highlights:
- Beautiful views of the Toronto skyline, especially during sunset.
- Extensive green space for picnics, playing sports, or just relaxing.
- Great place for fitness activities like jogging and running, with a full 400m track and a hill perfect for training.
- Close to Riverdale Farm, offering a unique, family-friendly farm experience in the city.
- Dog-friendly atmosphere, with plenty of space for dogs to exercise.

Restroom information: Public restrooms are available within Riverdale Farm during its operating hours (open until 5 pm). There are no dedicated restrooms in the park itself.

Recommendations: Ideal for those looking for a peaceful retreat in the city, a place to exercise, or simply enjoy the views. Pack a picnic, and be sure to visit the farm if you're bringing children along.

Taddle Creek Park
Location: 40 Bedford Rd, Toronto, ON M5R 2J9, Canada
Plus code: MJ92+WJ Toronto, Ontario, Canada
Contact: Not available
Website: www.toronto.ca
Opening hours: Daily: 7am – 11pm
Description:
Taddle Creek Park, located at 40 Bedford Road in Toronto, offers a small yet inviting green space in the Yorkville area. Just north of Bloor Street and near the University of Toronto, the park provides a peaceful respite for visitors. It features a playground that includes play structures for different age groups, a sandbox, swings, and a central sculpture called "The Vessel" by Ilan Sandler, which adds a unique artistic element to the park. A small oasis in the midst of a bustling city, Taddle Creek Park is dog-friendly, equipped with restrooms, and offers a picnic area for families and visitors to relax. The park is ideal for families with young children, with a secure play area that is easily supervised from nearby benches. Its proximity to major attractions like the Royal Ontario Museum and the Bata Shoe Museum makes it a convenient stop for those exploring the area. A nearby Starbucks and local eateries such as Trattoria Fieramosca offer convenient options for refreshments during a visit.

Nearby Attractions:
- Royal Ontario Museum (ROM)
- Bata Shoe Museum
- University of Toronto

Important Information for Visitors:
The park is small and often frequented by local families, so visitors should be prepared for a busy yet peaceful environment, particularly around the playground area. There is a single main entrance/exit to the park, making it easy to keep an eye on children. Be aware that while the park offers restrooms, they may be more basic in facilities.

Rouge National Urban Park

Location: 25 Zoo Rd, Toronto, ON M1B 5W8, Canada

Plus code: RR9G+5R Toronto, Ontario, Canada

Contact: +1 416-264-2020

Website: www.parks.canada.ca

Opening hours: Daily: 7:30am – 9pm

Description:

Rouge National Urban Park, located at 25 Zoo Road in Toronto, offers visitors a remarkable opportunity to experience the natural beauty of diverse landscapes including forests, meadows, wetlands, and the Rouge River. This expansive urban park provides a unique outdoor experience for nature lovers, with well-maintained trails such as the Vista and Mast Trails offering scenic views and a peaceful retreat from city life. The park is perfect for hiking, birdwatching, canoeing, fishing, and enjoying a picnic amidst serene surroundings. Accessible via public transportation (TTC), the park includes ample parking and washrooms near the entrance, ensuring convenience for all visitors. Be sure to bring insect repellent and your own water, as the park is rich in natural wilderness but short on supplies within its trails.

Rouge National Urban Park is highly recommended for solo visitors looking for reflection time, as well as families and friends seeking a quality outdoor experience. The park's scenic lookout points, including a must-see sunset view from the lookout, make for an unforgettable experience. Dogs are welcome in the park, provided they are leashed, making it a friendly spot for all. Note that the trails, particularly Mast Trail, may include some hills and log steps, which are not suitable for bikes or strollers. Parking is free, but it is advisable to arrive early as it fills up quickly, especially during peak times.

Nearby Attractions:

- Toronto Zoo
- Petticoat Creek Conservation Park

Important Information for Visitors:

Visitors are advised to bring insect repellent and their own drinks as amenities are limited along the trails. Wear appropriate footwear for hiking, as the trails are natural and include hills. Parking is free but limited, so early arrival is recommended.

TRAVEL

DATE:

DURATION:

DESTINATION:

PLACES TO SEE:

1 _____
2 _____
3 _____
4 _____
5 _____
6 _____
7 _____

LOCAL FOOD TO TRY:

1 _____
2 _____
3 _____
4 _____
5 _____
6 _____
7 _____

NOTES

EXPENSES IN TOTAL:

JOURNAL

Chorley Park
Location: 245 Douglas Dr, Toronto, ON M4W 2B9, Canada
Plus code: MJPJ+C7 Toronto, Ontario, Canada
Contact: +1 416-392-2489
Website: www.toronto.ca
Opening hours: Open 24 hours

Description: Chorley Park, located at 245 Douglas Drive in Toronto, is a serene 5-acre green space ideal for relaxation and quiet outdoor activities. The park is adorned with large, beautiful trees, offering plenty of shade and an inviting atmosphere for picnics, dog walks, and leisurely bike rides. There are several picnic tables and benches scattered around the park, providing ample seating for visitors looking to enjoy a meal or take in the peaceful surroundings. A notable feature of the park is the trail behind it, which leads to the Evergreen Brick Works, a popular nearby attraction. Though it involves a hike, the trail offers rewarding views and is well worth the effort.

Chorley Park is especially favored by dog owners, as it is a very dog-friendly space where pets are often seen off-leash. However, despite the regular presence of dogs, it remains a calm and tranquil area with little distraction, making it a perfect retreat for those seeking some quiet time. While the park does not have a playground, it is an excellent spot for families and kids of all ages to explore the natural beauty. Photographers also frequent the park, taking advantage of the stunning landscapes and views of the Brick Works.

Nearby Attractions:
- Evergreen Brick Works
- Rosedale Ravine Lands

Important Information for Visitors:
Chorley Park is a peaceful park with no playground, making it ideal for adults and families looking for a quiet outdoor space. The park connects to a trail leading to the Evergreen Brick Works. Dogs are often off-leash, so visitors who are uncomfortable with dogs should be aware.

Sheldon Lookout

Location: Martin Goodman Trl, Etobicoke, ON M8V 3W9, Canada

Plus code: JGJH+9C Etobicoke, Ontario, Canada

Contact: +1 416-392-2489

Website: www.toronto.ca

Opening hours: Daily: 6am – 11pm

Description: Sheldon Lookout, situated within Humber Bay Shores Park, offers a stunning panoramic view of the Toronto skyline. The lookout features several Muskoka chairs and small boulders where visitors can relax and take in the impressive cityscape, including the iconic CN Tower. It is an excellent spot for both daytime and nighttime visits, with clear views of the city and the Humber Bay Arch Bridge. The area is popular among walkers and bikers, with well-maintained trails providing scenic views of the Humber River and Lake Ontario.

The park is accessible from Parking Lot 207, which is free during the day. It is a short 30-minute walk from the parking area to the lookout. The site is mostly wheelchair accessible with paved walkways and offers a variety of seating options, including grass areas and break rocks. Although parking can be challenging, especially on sunny days, there are several nearby options and the experience is well worth the effort.

Nearby Attractions:
- Humber Bay Arch Bridge
- Humber Bay Shores Park

Important Information for Visitors:

Parking is available at Parking Lot 207, but can be limited on busy days. The lookout is accessible via paved pathways and offers ample seating, but it is advisable to visit earlier in the day or in the evening to avoid crowds.

Cherry Beach Clarke Beach Park

Location: 1 Cherry St, Toronto, ON M5A 0B7, Canada

Plus code: JMP4+P9 Toronto, Ontario, Canada

Contact: +1 416-338-4386

Website: www.toronto.ca

Opening hours: Daily: 5am – 11pm

Description: Cherry Beach Clarke Beach Park offers a serene escape from the bustle of downtown Toronto, featuring a tranquil beach setting that is less crowded compared to nearby Woodbine Beach. The park is known for its peaceful atmosphere, making it an ideal spot for leisurely strolls, picnicking, and enjoying a range of water sports such as paddle boarding, kayaking, and sailing. The beach is adjacent to Tom Thompson Park and provides access to a bike trail connecting it to the park, adding to its recreational appeal.

The park includes basic amenities such as restrooms and a food truck located in the main parking lot. While the water may not be suitable for swimming due to occasional weed presence and water quality, it remains a popular spot for walking and engaging in non-swimming water activities. Dogs are welcome, and there is a designated off-leash area, making it a great location for pet owners.

Nearby Attractions:
- Tom Thompson Park
- Humber Bay Shores Park

Important Information for Visitors:

The park is accessible by public transportation, and there is ample parking available. It is recommended to bring your own food and supplies as there are limited commercial amenities. Restrooms are available but may not always be well-maintained.

Trinity Bellwoods Park
Location: 790 Queen St W, Toronto, ON M6J 1G3, Canada
Plus code: JHWP+WG Toronto, Ontario, Canada
Website: www.trinitybellwoods.ca

Opening hours: Open 24 hours **Description:**
Trinity Bellwoods Park is a vibrant green space situated between Queen St W and Dundas St W in Toronto. Known for its beautifully landscaped grounds, the park is a favorite spot for picnics, relaxation, and community events. The park features a well-maintained playground equipped with a jungle gym, swings, and slides, making it ideal for families with young children. The off-leash dog area, located at the northern end of the park, is popular among pet owners.

The park is home to several amenities including tennis courts, a seasonal skating rink, and a splash pad for children. During the spring, visitors can enjoy the blooming cherry blossoms, and in the summer, the park hosts the "Art in the Park" summer camp for kids. There are ample picnic tables and grassy areas for lounging, and the park's open space accommodates various leisure activities such as frisbee and outdoor yoga classes.

Trinity Bellwoods Park fosters a strong sense of community, hosting events like the weekly farmer's market and providing a space where locals and visitors can connect. The park is also adjacent to the Trinity Community Recreation Centre, which offers additional facilities such as a swimming pool.

Nearby Attractions:
- Trinity Community Recreation Centre
- Queen Street West shopping district

Important Information for Visitors:
The park has public restrooms, but it is advisable to bring hand sanitizer and tissues. Alcohol consumption is permitted in the park, and visitors are encouraged to bring their own food and beverages. The park's central location makes it easily accessible by public transportation.

Riverdale Farm
Location: 201 Winchester St, Toronto, ON M4X 1B8, Canada
Plus code: MJ8Q+VH Toronto, Ontario, Canada
Contact: +1 416-392-6794
Website: www.riverdalefarmtoronto.ca
Opening hours:
- Thursday to Monday: 9 am – 5 pm
- Closed on Tuesdays and Wednesdays

Description: Riverdale Farm is a unique urban farm located in the heart of Toronto, offering a charming escape from city life. This free attraction features a range of farm animals including cows, goats, and sheep, making it an educational and enjoyable destination for families and children. The farm is designed with scenic paths and a pond, although the pond may occasionally be covered in algae.

The farm includes a small pool of water for children to play in during hot weather, and it also hosts occasional events on weekends. Despite its urban setting, Riverdale Farm provides a peaceful environment where visitors can experience farm life and connect with nature.

Visitors are encouraged to explore the farm's paths, which are designed to accommodate both leisurely strolls and educational exploration. Riverdale Farm is also connected to hiking trails, offering additional opportunities for outdoor activities.

Nearby Attractions:
- Riverdale Park (ideal for picnics)
- Necropolis Cemetery (historical site)

Important Information for Visitors:
- No bikes or dogs are allowed on the farm.
- Parking may be limited; street parking is available nearby.
- The farm's facilities include clean restrooms.
- The farm can be rented for birthday parties at a reasonable rate.

Edwards Gardens

Location: 755 Lawrence Ave E, North York, ON M3C 1P2, Canada
Plus Code: PJMR+GR North York, Ontario, Canada
Contact: +1 416-392-8188

Website: toronto.ca

Opening Hours:

- Monday to Sunday: 10 am – 8:30 pm

Description: Edwards Gardens is a botanical garden situated in the heart of Toronto, offering a serene retreat from the urban environment. Visitors can enjoy the extensive collection of plants and flowers, including beautifully landscaped gardens and unique large trees. The park features scenic trails along the river, ideal for hiking and leisurely walks. There are numerous picnic areas available, making it a great spot for family outings. The garden also has open spaces for children to play and a café where snacks and ice cream can be purchased.

The garden is easily accessible with ample parking available at a fee of $4 per hour or $8 for the maximum duration. Restrooms are located near the entrance. Dogs are permitted on leashes throughout the trails. Be mindful of mosquitoes near the water areas. The garden is especially vibrant during spring and fall, showcasing the best of its flora and fauna.

Nearby Attractions:

- The nearby Toronto Botanical Garden is adjacent to Edwards Gardens, offering additional plant displays and horticultural events.

Important Information for Visitors:

- Parking fees apply: $4 per hour or $8 for the maximum duration.
- The garden is free to enter.
- It is advisable to bring insect repellent if visiting during warmer months.

St. James Park
Location: 120 King St E,
Toronto, ON M5C 1G6, Canada
Plus Code: MJ2G+8Q Toronto,
Ontario, Canada
Contact: +1 416-392-2489
Website: toronto.ca

Opening Hours: Open 24 hours

Description: St. James Park is a picturesque urban park located in downtown Toronto, adjacent to St. James Cathedral. The park features well-maintained paths, mature trees, and vibrant floral displays that provide a serene escape in the city. Key highlights include a small circular fountain with surrounding seating and a children's playground with a market-themed design, including playful elements like asparagus and carrots, swings, slides, and climbing walls.

Although the park has limited picnic facilities with only two picnic tables, there are numerous benches available for relaxation. The park's proximity to various bars, restaurants, and the historic St. James Cathedral enhances its appeal as a convenient and charming place to unwind. Dogs are allowed on the lawn, provided their waste is cleaned up. The park's location also offers pleasant views of the CN Tower and is an ideal spot to enjoy a book or have conversations in a peaceful setting.

Nearby Attractions:
- St. James Cathedral
- The St. Lawrence Market
- Numerous local bars and restaurants

Important Information for Visitors:
- No public restrooms are available in the park.
- Parking may be limited; consider using public transportation or nearby parking facilities.

Princes' Gates

Location: 11 Princes' Blvd, Toronto, ON M6K 3C3, Canada
Plus Code: JHMR+V5 Toronto, Ontario, Canada
Contact: Not applicable
Website: explace.on.ca
Opening Hours: Open 24 hours

Description: Princes' Gates is a historic and grand archway located at the east entrance of Exhibition Place in Toronto. Constructed in the late 19th century, this ceremonial archway features intricate Victorian architecture and commemorates the royal visit of the Duke of Wales and Prince George. The gates are a significant symbol of Toronto's progress and have been a witness to numerous important events in the city's history. The architectural design includes detailed sculptures, including an angel at the top, and symbolic pillars representing different provinces. The site is a popular spot for photos and serves as a prominent landmark during events held at Exhibition Place, such as the Canadian National Exhibition.

Nearby Attractions:
- Exhibition Place
- The Canadian National Exhibition (CNE)

Important Information for Visitors:
- The Princes' Gates are accessible 24 hours a day.
- No reservations are needed to visit the gates.
- The area is typically bustling during major events, so plan your visit accordingly.

Allan Gardens

Location: 160 Gerrard St E, Toronto, ON M5A 2E5, Canada
Plus Code: MJ6G+M4 Toronto, Ontario, Canada
Contact: +1 416-392-7288
Website: toronto.ca

Opening Hours:
- Thursday to Tuesday: 10 am – 5 pm
- Closed on Wednesdays

Description: Allan Gardens is a tranquil botanical oasis located in downtown Toronto. The gardens feature a series of greenhouses that showcase a diverse collection of plants, including vibrant flowers, succulents, and cacti. The indoor environment provides a warm and inviting escape, especially during the winter months. The gardens are renowned for their meticulously designed floral displays and lush greenery. Adjacent to the gardens is a park area with benches, although visitors should be aware that the park may have a noticeable presence of homeless individuals, which might affect the ambiance for some. Additionally, there is a playground situated just outside the gardens. The facility is operated by the City of Toronto and offers free admission. It is an ideal spot for plant enthusiasts and those seeking a peaceful retreat from the city's hustle and bustle. After visiting, guests can enjoy a coffee and snacks at the nearby Bulldog Cafe.

Nearby Attractions:
- Bulldog Cafe

Important Information for Visitors:
- Free admission to the gardens.
- The gardens are closed on Wednesdays.
- Limited accessibility in certain areas due to ongoing construction/renovations.

Toronto Botanical Garden
Location: 777 Lawrence Ave E, Toronto, ON M3C 1P2, Canada
Plus Code: PJMR+MP Toronto, Ontario, Canada
Contact: +1 416-397-1341
Website: torontobotanicalgarden.ca
Opening Hours:
- Open 24 hours, daily

Description: The Toronto Botanical Garden is a picturesque green space offering a serene escape within the city. The garden features meticulously maintained floral displays, diverse plant collections, and scenic walking paths. It is situated alongside

Wilket Creek and Sunnybrook Park, enhancing its natural charm with abundant local wildlife. Visitors can enjoy various garden areas, relax on numerous benches, and explore the tranquil surroundings. The garden also has a cozy café, perfect for grabbing a coffee and enjoying the views. Admission is free, though there is a parking fee of $4 per hour. Free parking is available along the side of Sunnybrook Park. The garden is a popular destination year-round, with each season showcasing its own unique beauty.

Nearby Attractions:
- Wilket Creek Park
- Sunnybrook Park

Important Information for Visitors:
- Free admission to the gardens.
- Parking costs $4 per hour, with free parking options available at Sunnybrook Park.
- The gardens are open 24 hours, but the café and some facilities have specific hours.

TRAVEL

DATE:

DURATION:

DESTINATION:

PLACES TO SEE:

1 _____
2 _____
3 _____
4 _____
5 _____
6 _____
7 _____

LOCAL FOOD TO TRY:

1 _____
2 _____
3 _____
4 _____
5 _____
6 _____
7 _____

NOTES

EXPENSES IN TOTAL:

JOURNAL

Toronto Inukshuk Park

Location: 789 Lake Shore Blvd W, Toronto, ON M5V 3T7, Canada
Plus Code: JHJR+X5 Toronto, Ontario, Canada
Contact: +1 416-338-4386
Website: toronto.ca
Opening Hours: Open 24 hours, daily

Description: Toronto Inukshuk Park is notable for its impressive Inukshuk, one of the largest stone structures of its kind in North America. Standing approximately 9 meters tall and crafted from mountain rose granite, this monument is a significant symbol of Canada's First Nations. Located within Coronation Park, the Inukshuk provides a striking focal point against the backdrop of Lake Ontario and the Toronto skyline. The park itself serves as a connector between Coronation Park and Trillium Park, offering green space and pathways ideal for walking and cycling. Visitors can enjoy scenic views of Billy Bishop Airport and the lake, making it a popular spot for photography and outdoor activities. Ample parking is available nearby, and the area is particularly lively in the summer, attracting bikers, runners, and families. The park's proximity to Ontario Place and the waterfront enhances its appeal, though it can become crowded during peak seasons.

Nearby Attractions:
- Coronation Park
- Trillium Park
- Ontario Place

Important Information for Visitors:
- Open 24 hours, daily.
- Parking is available adjacent to the park.
- Be prepared for crowds during peak seasons, particularly in summer.

Berczy Park
Location: 35 Wellington St E, Toronto, ON M5E 1C6, Canada
Plus Code: JJXF+6W Toronto, Ontario, Canada
Contact: +1 416-338-4386
Website: toronto.ca
Opening Hours:

- Open 24 hours, daily

Description: Berczy Park, situated in downtown Toronto, is a cherished green space named after William Berczy, a notable early settler and artist. This 1.25-acre park is renowned for its distinctive dog fountain, designed by Canadian artist Claude Cormier. The fountain features 27 cast-iron dog sculptures of various breeds, along with cats and other animals, creating a playful and engaging centerpiece. The park also includes a splash pad, playground, open lawn areas, and multiple seating options under a canopy of trees. Located near the St. Lawrence Market and the Flat Iron Building, it offers a vibrant atmosphere ideal for relaxation, picnicking, and people-watching. Its well-maintained gardens, open spaces, and community-oriented events make it a popular spot for both locals and visitors. The park's convenient location and range of amenities make it a valuable urban retreat.

Nearby Attractions:
- St. Lawrence Market
- Flat Iron Building

Important Information for Visitors:
- Open 24 hours, daily.
- The park is popular and can get busy, particularly during peak times.
- Seating is available, but it can be crowded.
- The park is a short walk from various restaurants and bars, ideal for grabbing a bite before or after your visit.

HTO Park

Location: 339 Queens Quay W, Toronto, ON M5V 1A2, Canada

Plus Code: JJQ6+4P Toronto, Ontario, Canada

Contact: +1 416-392-8188

Website: toronto.ca

Opening Hours:
- Open 24 hours, daily

Description: HTO Park offers a scenic waterfront retreat on Lake Ontario, perfect for relaxation and recreation. The park features a sandy beach, lush green spaces, and expansive areas for picnicking. It provides stunning views of the Toronto skyline and the Toronto Islands, making it a popular spot for both locals and visitors. The park includes ample seating, mobile restrooms, and is well-connected by streetcar with Union Station within walking distance. During the summer, the area is bustling with water activities, including cruises and water taxis, as well as opportunities for cycling, kayaking, and canoeing. In winter, the park transforms into a tranquil spot to enjoy the serene lake views. HTO Park's location near various restaurants and its picturesque setting make it a desirable destination for a leisurely day out.

Nearby Attractions:
- Toronto Islands
- CN Tower
- Union Station

Important Information for Visitors:
- Open 24 hours, daily.
- Mobile restrooms are available.
- The park is busy during summer, especially with water activities and nearby cruise operations.
- It is easily accessible via streetcar, and Union Station is within walking distance.

Liberty Village Park

Location: 70 E Liberty St, Toronto, ON M6K 3K7, Canada
Plus Code: JHQP+G4 Toronto, Ontario, Canada
Contact: +1 416-392-2489
Website: toronto.ca
Opening Hours:

• Open 24 hours, daily

Description: Liberty Village Park is a charming green space located in the heart of the vibrant Liberty Village neighborhood in Toronto. This small park provides a refreshing escape from the surrounding urban environment and is popular with both local residents and visitors. It features open grassy areas ideal for children and dogs, and there are a few unique elements such as hammock-like seating structures. The park is surrounded by a revitalized neighborhood that includes historic buildings, modern condos, and various amenities like restaurants, coffee shops, and retail stores.

The park does not have washroom facilities, and it can become muddy after rain due to its clay-like soil and high foot traffic. Despite this, it remains a favored spot for relaxation and leisure, especially among dog owners and families with young children. The park's historical context, including its past as an industrial site and the presence of the old house undergoing restoration, adds to its unique character.

Nearby Attractions:

- Liberty Market Village
- Exhibition Place (CNE)
- Toronto Carpet Factory

Important Information for Visitors:

- The park is open 24 hours, but may become muddy after rain.
- No washroom facilities on-site.
- Popular with local residents, especially dog owners and families.

Sunnyside Park
Location: 2001 Lake Shore Blvd W, Toronto, ON M6K 1L4, Canada
Plus Code: JGMJ+QR Toronto, Ontario, Canada
Contact: +1 416-392-2489
Website: toronto.ca
Opening Hours:

- Open 24 hours, daily

Description: Sunnyside Park, located within Sir Casimir Gzowski Park, is a bustling and popular spot along Toronto's waterfront. The park features a lively beach area, ideal for those who enjoy a vibrant atmosphere. On weekends, it can become quite crowded, making parking a challenge, but it offers a range of amenities and activities that attract visitors.

Features:

- **Beach:** A lovely sandy beach that is a popular destination in the summer. Note that it can be very crowded.
- **Picnic Areas:** There are picnic tables and BBQ spots, though it can get crowded.
- **Playground:** Includes a playground area for children and a shallow waiting pool.
- **Splash Pad:** A fun water feature for kids.
- **Bike Track & Trails:** Suitable for biking and walking.
- **Dog Park:** There is a fenced dog park for pets.
- **Restrooms:** Available at the park.
- **Historical Pavilion:** The pavilion has historical significance as a gathering spot for swimming in Lake Ontario over a century ago.

Historical Note: The pool at the park is named after Gus Ryder, who was the trainer for Marilyn Bell, the first woman to swim across Lake Ontario.

Important Information for Visitors:

- **Crowds:** The park can get extremely busy, especially on weekends.
- **Parking:** Finding parking may be difficult during peak times.
- **Dog-Friendly:** There is a fenced area for dogs.

Nearby Attractions:

- Lake Ontario waterfront
- Bike and walking trails along the lake

Budapest Park

Location: 1575 Lake Shore Blvd W, Toronto, ON M6K 3C1, Canada

Plus Code: JHP2+R3 Toronto, Ontario, Canada

Contact: +1 416-338-4386

Website:  toronto.ca

Opening Hours:

• Open 24 hours, daily

Description: Budapest Park is a scenic spot along Toronto's waterfront, known for its beautiful trail and vibrant atmosphere. It offers a mix of relaxation and recreational activities with stunning views of the lake.

Features:

• **Trail:** A pleasant trail along the water, ideal for walking and jogging. It's long enough to make a round trip of about 10,000 steps.

- **Playground:** Available for children.
- **Public Restrooms:** Yes, though some reviews mention they could be cleaner.
- **Picnic Tables:** Yes, suitable for eating and relaxing.
- **Barbecue Grills:** No.
- **Dog Area:** No off-leash dog area.

Notable Points:

- **Atmosphere:** The park is popular for its refreshing breezes and vibrant beach area, though it can get crowded in the summer.
- **Shade:** Plenty of trees provide shade, making it a comfortable spot on hot days.
- **Accessibility:** Easy parking and access to the waterfront.

Visitor Tips:

- **Crowds:** The beach area can be filled with people, particularly on hot days.
- **Maintenance:** Some visitors have noted that the park could benefit from more regular upkeep, especially concerning dry grass and restroom cleanliness.
- **Safety:** Be aware of your surroundings, especially in areas where there might be unsavory characters.

Nearby Attractions:
- Humber Bridge
- Other waterfront trails and beaches

Ireland Park
Location: Eireann Quay, Toronto, ON M5V 3G3, Canada
Plus Code: JJM3+WP Toronto, Ontario, Canada
Contact: +1 416-601-6906
Website: canadairelandfoundation.com
Opening Hours:
- Open 24 hours, daily

Description: Ireland Park is a commemorative park located on Toronto's waterfront, dedicated to the Irish immigrants who arrived during the Great Famine. The park features a series of poignant bronze statues that reflect the hardships and hopes of these early settlers.

Features:
- **Statues:** The park showcases a series of five bronze statues representing the arrival of Irish immigrants. The statues include a range of figures from emaciated individuals to a skeletal pregnant woman and a child. These sculptures are a solemn tribute to the tragic conditions endured by the immigrants.
- **View:** Offers a serene lake view and is particularly beautiful during autumn.
- **Historical Context:** The park commemorates the Irish immigrants who fled the Great Famine, highlighting the challenges they faced and their significant impact on Toronto.

Notable Points:
- **Atmosphere:** The park provides a reflective and solemn atmosphere, making it ideal for contemplation and understanding the historical significance of Irish immigration.
- **Maintenance:** Some visitors have noted that the park has faced maintenance issues, especially due to nearby construction. However, it remains a meaningful site for those interested in Irish heritage.

- **Visibility:** The park is somewhat hidden and may be easily missed due to ongoing construction and its location off the beaten path.

Visitor Tips:
- **Location:** It may be worth visiting the park for its historical and reflective value, but be aware of possible construction and maintenance issues.
- **Events:** The park is known for offering a unique vantage point for viewing New Year's Eve fireworks in Toronto.
- **Cleanliness:** Some reviews mention that the park has faced issues with litter and disrepair, though these concerns have been addressed to some extent over time.

Nearby Attractions:
- **Billy Bishop Toronto City Airport:** Close by for those interested in aviation.
- **Martin Goodman Trail:** A waterfront trail that runs near the park, offering additional recreational opportunities.

Little Norway Park
Location: 659 Queens Quay W, Toronto, ON M5V 3N2, Canada
Plus Code: JJP2+3F Toronto, Ontario, Canada
Contact: +1 416-392-2489
Opening Hours:
• Open 24 hours, daily

Description: Little Norway Park is a quaint green space located near Toronto's waterfront. The park offers a serene retreat with picturesque views of Lake Ontario and the Toronto Islands, making it ideal for a relaxed outing.

Features:
- **Scenic Views:** Provides beautiful views of Lake Ontario, the Toronto Islands, and Billy Bishop Airport, where visitors can watch planes land and take off.
- **Playground:** Includes a playground suitable for young children with a net climbing structure for slightly older kids.

- **Green Spaces:** Lush, well-maintained grassy areas for picnics and leisurely strolls.
- **Unique Features:** The park features a charming arbour and a distinctive metal balcony overlooking a grassy area.

Notable Points:
- **Serene Atmosphere:** Offers a peaceful escape from the busy city, with less foot traffic compared to some other waterfront parks.
- **Hidden Gem:** Often described as an underrated park, it provides a more tranquil experience compared to other crowded areas.
- **Restrooms:** Recent reviews indicate issues with restroom facilities, including encampments and cleanliness problems. Porta potties on site are reportedly in poor condition.

Visitor Tips:
- **Best Times to Visit:** Early morning or late afternoon can offer the best views and a quieter experience.
- **Safety Concerns:** Recent reports highlight issues with encampments and safety. It's advisable to be cautious, especially around the restrooms and less frequented areas.
- **Accessibility:** The park is close to the Billy Bishop Toronto Island Airport, making it a convenient spot to visit if you're in the area.

Nearby Attractions:
- **Billy Bishop Toronto Island Airport:** Provides a close-up view of the airport's operations.
- **Harbourfront Area:** Just east of Little Norway Park, this area offers additional recreational and cultural activities.

Village of Yorkville Park
Location: 115 Cumberland St, Toronto, ON M5S 2W7, Canada
Plus Code: MJC5+28 Toronto, Ontario, Canada
Contact: +1 416-338-4386
Opening Hours:

- Open 24 hours, daily

Description: Village of Yorkville Park is a charming urban oasis situated in the vibrant Yorkville neighborhood of Toronto. Despite its central location, the park offers a cozy and tranquil retreat amidst the bustling city.

Features:

- **Picnic Areas:** Equipped with seating and tables, making it a pleasant spot for a meal. Be mindful of the pigeons that might join you!
- **Events:** Hosts a variety of seasonal events and festivals, including the Cavalcade of Lights during winter and ice sculpture festivals in February.
- **Scenic Beauty:** Surrounded by upscale restaurants and shopping outlets, the park offers a mix of natural beauty and urban vibrancy.
- **Art and History:** Features a prominent boulder that is over a billion years old, and various sections with unique designs and landscaping.

Notable Points:

- **Seasonal Attractions:** The park transforms during different times of the year. In winter, it becomes a Winter Wonderland with Christmas lights and ice sculptures.
- **Central Location:** Right in the heart of Yorkville, it is easily accessible and close to many dining and shopping options.
- **Family-Friendly:** A great spot for families, especially during special events and festivals.

Visitor Tips:

- **Best Times to Visit:** Winter for the festive lights and ice sculptures; spring and summer for pleasant weather and vibrant surroundings.
- **Crowds:** The park can get busy during events and festivals, so plan your visit accordingly if you prefer a quieter experience.
- **Parking and Accessibility:** Located above Bay subway station, making it easily accessible by public transport.

Nearby Attractions:

- **Yorkville Village:** Explore the nearby shops, cafes, and restaurants.
- **Bloor Street:** A major shopping street with a wide variety of stores and boutiques.

- **Royal Ontario Museum:** A short walk away, offering additional cultural and historical exploration.

Little India
Location: 1426 Gerrard Street (East), From Glenside Ave. to Coxwell Ave., Toronto, ON M4L 1Z6, Canada
Contact: +1 416-465-8513
Hours:
- **Thursday-Sunday:** 9 AM – 2 AM
- **Monday:** 9 AM – 2 AM
- **Tuesday:** Closed
- **Wednesday:** 9 AM – 2 AM

Description: Little India is a vibrant neighborhood in Toronto known for its South Asian community and cultural offerings. The area is characterized by a variety of ethnic shops, restaurants, and cultural experiences.

Features:
- **Food:** Offers a wide range of South Asian cuisine, with a notable variety of Indian and Pakistani restaurants. While some diners find it a great place to explore diverse food options, others have reported mixed experiences with food quality and spiciness levels.
- **Shops:** Includes stores selling Indian and South Asian items, though some visitors have found the clothing shops to be outdated.
- **Cultural Experience:** Provides an authentic South Asian cultural atmosphere, making it a unique experience in Toronto.

Visitor Tips:
- **Food Recommendations:** Be cautious when selecting restaurants; some places are well-regarded while others might not meet expectations. If you have specific spice preferences, be sure to communicate them clearly.
- **Safety and Cleanliness:** The area has had mixed reviews regarding cleanliness and safety. It's advised to stay aware of your surroundings and exercise caution, especially in certain spots.
- **Parking:** Street parking can be challenging, so consider looking for parking in nearby side streets.

- **Accessibility:** The area is accessible by streetcar but lacks direct TTC subway access.

Nearby Attractions:
- **Gerrard Street:** Explore the variety of shops and eateries along this street.
- **Toronto's Downtown:** For a broader selection of dining and cultural experiences, consider venturing into downtown Toronto.

Overall: Little India provides a unique cultural experience with its South Asian influences but comes with some caveats regarding food quality and safety. It can be a worthwhile visit for those interested in exploring diverse cuisines and cultural elements.

TRAVEL

DATE:

DURATION:

DESTINATION:

PLACES TO SEE:

1 _____
2 _____
3 _____
4 _____
5 _____
6 _____
7 _____

LOCAL FOOD TO TRY:

1 _____
2 _____
3 _____
4 _____
5 _____
6 _____
7 _____

NOTES

EXPENSES IN TOTAL:

JOURNAL

The Ravine with Moccasin Identifier

Location: 955 Lake Shore Blvd W, Toronto, ON M6K 3B9, Canada (Located in Trillium Park)

Contact: ontarioplace.com

Hours:
- **Monday-Sunday:** 6 AM – 11 PM

Description: The Ravine with Moccasin Identifier is a scenic area within Trillium Park, offering a blend of natural beauty and cultural elements. The park features trails and viewpoints, as well as interpretive elements like the Moccasin Identifier, which highlights Indigenous heritage.

Features:
- **Trails:** The park includes trails with varying conditions. The starting point is steep, which might not be suitable for strollers or wheelchairs. Some parts of the trail can be slushy, muddy, and have broken trees and branches.
- **Scenic Views:** Provides beautiful views of Toronto and the surrounding natural landscape.
- **Cultural Element:** The Moccasin Identifier is a feature that reflects Indigenous culture, providing educational information about local heritage.

Visitor Tips:
- **Accessibility:** Be prepared for a challenging start to the trail. It may be difficult for those with mobility issues or young children in strollers.
- **Parking:** Available on the street or in a nearby plaza.
- **Condition:** The trail can be noisy due to its proximity to the highway, and some sections may be less well-maintained, so wear appropriate footwear.

Nearby Attractions:
- **Trillium Park:** Explore the wider park area, which includes other trails and natural features.
- **Ontario Place:** The park is part of Ontario Place, which offers additional attractions and activities.

Overall: The Ravine with Moccasin Identifier is a picturesque spot with educational elements. While it offers stunning views and a connection to Indigenous culture, visitors should be aware of the trail's accessibility challenges and varying conditions.

The Pasture
Location: 100 The PATH - Canadian Pacific Tower- Wellington, Toronto, ON M5K 2A1, Canada (Located in Toronto-Dominion Centre)

Description: The Pasture is an urban green space situated in the heart of downtown Toronto. This charming area features seven bronze cows, all identical, which add a unique and whimsical touch to the park. It offers a peaceful respite from the bustling city environment.

Features:

- **Bronze Sculptures:** The highlight of The Pasture is the set of seven identical bronze cows lounging on the grass, creating a whimsical and calming atmosphere.
- **Picnic Area:** Well-maintained lawns and picnic tables are available, providing a pleasant spot for a meal or relaxation.
- **Quiet Spot:** A tranquil space amidst the busy downtown area, perfect for contemplation, a break, or admiring the surrounding architecture.

Visitor Tips:

- **Enjoy the Art:** Take a moment to appreciate the quirky bronze sculptures and the serene setting.
- **Relax and Unwind:** The area is ideal for a quiet lunch or a peaceful pause during a busy day.
- **Picnic:** Bring some snacks or a meal to enjoy at one of the tables in this well-kept space.

Overall: The Pasture offers a unique blend of art and nature in a serene downtown setting, making it a perfect spot to escape the city's chaos and enjoy a moment of tranquility.

Harbour Square Park

Location: 25 Queens Quay W, Toronto, ON M5J 2G4, Canada

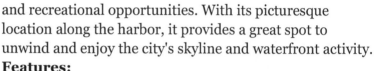
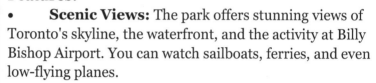

Description: Harbour Square Park is a vibrant waterfront park in downtown Toronto, offering a mix of scenic views and recreational opportunities. With its picturesque location along the harbor, it provides a great spot to unwind and enjoy the city's skyline and waterfront activity.

Features:

- **Scenic Views:** The park offers stunning views of Toronto's skyline, the waterfront, and the activity at Billy Bishop Airport. You can watch sailboats, ferries, and even low-flying planes.
- **Recreational Opportunities:** Ideal for walking, skating, or taking your dog for a stroll. The park is well-suited for outdoor activities and relaxation.
- **Picnic Areas:** Popular for picnics, especially on weekends when the park can get busy with families and groups enjoying the outdoors.
- **Children's Play Areas:** Nearby parks for children add to the family-friendly atmosphere.
- **Art and Vibe:** The park features free art installations and a pleasant vibe, making it a nice spot to sit and relax by the water.

Visitor Tips:

- **Great for Walks:** The park is perfect for a leisurely walk or bike ride, especially on a nice summer day.
- **Enjoy the Waterfront:** Sit by the water to enjoy the views of boats, cruise ships, and the occasional duck family.
- **Relax and Unwind:** Take a break from the city bustle and enjoy a cold drink at one of the nearby pubs or simply relax by the water.

Overall: Harbour Square Park is a delightful urban oasis that offers beautiful views, recreational activities, and a relaxing atmosphere, making it a popular spot for both locals and visitors.

CN Tower

Location: 290 Bremner Blvd, Toronto, ON M5V 3L9, Canada
Plus Code: JJV7+25 Toronto, Ontario, Canada
Contact: +1 416-868-6937
Website: www.cntower.ca
Opening Hours:
 Monday to Sunday: 9:30 am – 9:30 pm

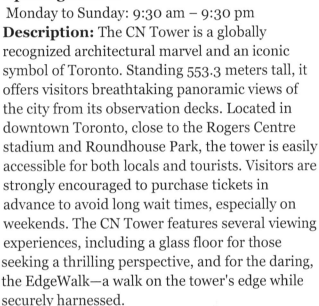

Description: The CN Tower is a globally recognized architectural marvel and an iconic symbol of Toronto. Standing 553.3 meters tall, it offers visitors breathtaking panoramic views of the city from its observation decks. Located in downtown Toronto, close to the Rogers Centre stadium and Roundhouse Park, the tower is easily accessible for both locals and tourists. Visitors are strongly encouraged to purchase tickets in advance to avoid long wait times, especially on weekends. The CN Tower features several viewing experiences, including a glass floor for those seeking a thrilling perspective, and for the daring, the EdgeWalk—a walk on the tower's edge while securely harnessed.

The 360° Restaurant provides a fine dining experience with rotating views of the city, adding a unique culinary experience to your visit. At the base of the tower, the Toronto Aquarium offers an engaging experience with exhibits of marine life including sharks, stingrays, and turtles. Parking is available across the street in a paid lot, ensuring convenience for visitors. The CN Tower is a must-visit destination in Toronto, offering not only stunning views but also opportunities for adventure and relaxation.

Nearby Attractions:
- Ripley's Aquarium of Canada
- Rogers Centre
- Roundhouse Park

Important Information for Visitors:
It is highly recommended to book tickets in advance to avoid long queues.
The tower can get crowded, especially during weekends and events at
nearby locations such as the Rogers Centre.

Toronto Sign
Location: 100 Queen St W, Toronto,
ON M5H 2N2, Canada
Plus Code: MJ28+WH Toronto,
Ontario, Canada
Contact: +1 416-392-2489
Website: www.toronto.ca
Opening Hours: Open 24 hours
Description:
The Toronto Sign at Nathan Phillips Square is a vibrant
and iconic landmark that represents the heart of the
city. Situated in the bustling square outside City Hall,
the sign has become a must-visit spot for tourists and
locals alike. Day or night, it serves as a perfect
backdrop for photos, offering a lively atmosphere filled
with energy, live music, and nearby food trucks
offering global cuisines. At night, the sign is illuminated in stunning
colors, creating a mesmerizing sight. Nathan Phillips Square itself provides
ample space for relaxation, with seating areas, a fountain, and a clean,
well-maintained environment. During certain events, the square can
become crowded, but generally, it remains an accessible and enjoyable
spot to visit. Parking nearby can range from $20-$40 for the day. For a
truly unique experience, visiting the Toronto Sign at night is highly
recommended.
Nearby Attractions:
- City Hall
- Eaton Centre
- Yonge-Dundas Square

Important Information for Visitors:
Public restrooms in the area may be less than ideal, and during events, the
area can become crowded. Parking can be expensive, so plan accordingly.

Roundhouse Park

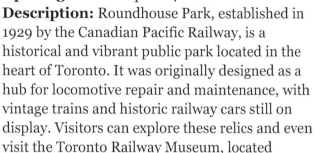

Location: 255 Bremner Blvd, Toronto, ON M5V 3M9, Canada

Plus Code: JJR7+GV Toronto, Ontario, Canada

Contact: +1 416-214-9229

Website: www.trha.ca

Opening Hours: Open 24 hours

Description: Roundhouse Park, established in 1929 by the Canadian Pacific Railway, is a historical and vibrant public park located in the heart of Toronto. It was originally designed as a hub for locomotive repair and maintenance, with vintage trains and historic railway cars still on display. Visitors can explore these relics and even visit the Toronto Railway Museum, located within the park. The park also features open green spaces ideal for picnics, a children's playground, and a miniature train ride that operates in the summer.

Roundhouse Park offers a variety of attractions for both locals and tourists. The Steam Whistle Brewery, situated on-site, is a popular stop for beer enthusiasts, while a couple of restaurants add to the appeal of the area. The park is dog-friendly, though dogs should remain on a leash. Located near other major attractions like the CN Tower, Ripley's Aquarium, and Rogers Centre stadium, it is a great spot for sightseeing or relaxing. Visitors are advised that the public areas may occasionally be less well-maintained, but the charm and history of the park still make it worth a visit.

Nearby Attractions:

- CN Tower
- Ripley's Aquarium of Canada
- Rogers Centre Stadium
- Toronto Railway Museum
- Steam Whistle Brewery

Important Information for Visitors:

Restroom access can be limited, but Steam Whistle Brewery typically allows visitors to use their facilities. Keep dogs leashed in the park, and note that maintenance in some areas could be improved.

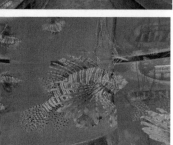

Ripley's Aquarium of Canada
Location: 288 Bremner Blvd, Toronto, ON M5V 3L9, Canada
Plus Code: JJR7+V9 Toronto, Ontario, Canada
Contact: +1 647-351-3474
Website: www.ripleyaquariums.com

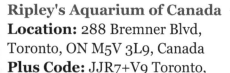

Opening Hours: Friday to Thursday: 9 am – 11 pm
Description: Ripley's Aquarium of Canada is one of Toronto's most popular attractions, offering a captivating experience for visitors of all ages. Located near the CN Tower and Rogers Centre, this world-class aquarium showcases a wide range of marine life from across the globe, including both saltwater and freshwater species. Highlights include the mesmerizing underwater tunnel where you can view sharks and rays swimming overhead, as well as interactive touch pools where visitors can get up close to stingrays and other sea creatures. The jellyfish exhibit, with its colorful and glowing displays, is also a crowd favorite.

The aquarium is well-maintained, with exhibits designed to both educate and entertain. It is highly recommended to purchase tickets in advance to avoid long wait times, especially during weekends and holidays when it can get very crowded. Despite the crowds, the aquarium remains a fantastic place to explore the wonders of marine life, offering several interactive zones for children and a fun play area to keep younger visitors engaged.

Visitors should be aware that navigating the aquarium can be challenging during peak hours due to narrow walkways and large crowds, making it less accessible for those with mobility needs. The aquarium also features a gift shop with a wide range of souvenirs and a food court, although it can get busy during peak hours. Overall, Ripley's Aquarium is a must-see for anyone visiting Toronto, providing a unique and memorable experience for families and individuals alike.

Nearby Attractions:

- CN Tower
- Rogers Centre Stadium
- Roundhouse Park
- Steam Whistle Brewery
- Toronto Railway Museum

Important Information for Visitors:

Presto cardholders can enjoy discounts on admission. Be prepared for crowds during peak times, and strollers may be difficult to manage due to the density of visitors.

Spadina Museum

Location: 285 Spadina Rd, Toronto, ON M5R 2V5, Canada
Plus Code: MHHR+HP Toronto, Ontario, Canada
Contact: +1 416-392-6910
Website: www.toronto.ca
Opening Hours:

- Friday to Sunday: 11 am – 5 pm
- Monday to Tuesday: Closed
- Wednesday to Thursday: 11 am – 5 pm

Description: Spadina Museum is a beautifully preserved historical mansion in Toronto, offering visitors a glimpse into the lifestyle of a wealthy Canadian family from the 19th and 20th centuries. This charming estate, located next to Casa Loma, showcases the design, art, and intimate details of life during the time through its well-curated interiors and artifacts. The museum is free to enter and often offers guided tours that enhance the experience by diving into the history and stories behind the family who lived there.

The mansion is surrounded by lush gardens and parkland, making it a lovely spot for a peaceful stroll, a picnic, or even a nap under the trees. The gardens feature beautiful greenery, flowers, and fruit trees, providing a tranquil environment in the heart of the city. Many visitors appreciate the relaxing atmosphere of the grounds, as well as the opportunity to explore the rich history of the home itself.

Tours can last up to 90 minutes, and it's recommended to arrive early in the day to fully enjoy the museum and gardens. The staff is known for being knowledgeable and friendly, making each visit informative and enjoyable. While the museum itself is not large, the wealth of detail and history presented makes it a rewarding experience for history enthusiasts and curious visitors alike.

Nearby Attractions:

- Casa Loma
- Baldwin Steps
- Wells Hill Park
- Sir Winston Churchill Park

Visitor Tips:

- No reservations are needed, but tours can book up quickly on weekends.
- The mansion has no on-site parking, but parking is available at Casa Loma, which is within walking distance.
- The outdoor gardens are particularly lovely on sunny days and are perfect for a picnic or casual stroll.

Allen Lambert Galleria

Location: 181 Bay St., Toronto, ON M5J 2T3, Canada
Floor: 1, Brookfield Place
Contact: +1 416-777-6480
Description:

The Allen Lambert Galleria is an iconic architectural landmark located within Brookfield Place in Toronto's financial district. Designed by renowned architect Santiago Calatrava, the galleria's stunning six-story high structure is often described as a "crystal cathedral of commerce." Its soaring white arches create a canopy effect that resembles a forest, making it a popular destination for photographers, tourists, and architecture enthusiasts alike.

The space is frequently used for art exhibitions and events, adding to its vibrant and cultural atmosphere. One of the highlights is the floor with lit glass tiles, which gives the galleria a unique glow, particularly at night. Despite being located in the heart of the bustling financial district, the galleria offers a serene environment, making it a great spot for relaxation, casual strolls, or enjoying a cup of coffee while taking in the remarkable surroundings.

The Allen Lambert Galleria is also connected to the Hockey Hall of Fame, making it a convenient stop for visitors looking to combine architectural appreciation with a bit of Canadian sports history. Though the galleria sees regular foot traffic from office workers and visitors, it remains accessible and welcoming, with plenty of seating areas to unwind and admire the design.

Visitor Tips:
- Photography is allowed, but tripods are not permitted due to security policies.
- Best visited during the day for natural light or at night when the lit tiles enhance the ambiance.
- Nearby attractions include the Hockey Hall of Fame and Brookfield Place's food court, offering a range of dining options.

Nearby Attractions:
- Hockey Hall of Fame
- Scotiabank Arena
- St. Lawrence Market
- Toronto's Financial District

Museum of Illusions Toronto
Location: 132 Front St E, Toronto, ON M5A 1E2, Canada
Plus code: MJ2J+24 Toronto, Ontario, Canada
Contact: +1 416-889-2285
Website: www.museumofillusions.ca
Opening hours: Monday to Sunday: 10 am – 9 pm
Description:
The Museum of Illusions in Toronto offers a captivating and fun experience with a variety of

illusions that challenge your perceptions and stimulate your mind. Located in the core of downtown, the museum features numerous interactive exhibits and photo opportunities, making it ideal for visitors of all ages. Popular attractions include the room where you can change sizes and several mirrored illusions. Visitors are highly recommended to ask staff for tips on how to capture the best photos and fully engage with the illusions. While the museum is compact, you can comfortably explore its exhibits in under an hour. This attraction is well-suited for a quick, entertaining stop during your visit to Toronto. Nearby attractions include the Hockey Hall of Fame and other cultural and shopping spots in the bustling downtown area.

Important Information for Visitors:

- Reservations are recommended, especially on weekends, to avoid long waits.
- The museum is LGBTQ+ friendly and welcomes all visitors.
- Note that the space can be smaller than expected, so it is advised to plan accordingly for a brief visit.

Toronto Skyline View
Location: Ferry Dock, Toronto, ON M5J, Canada
Plus code: JJJR+JV Toronto, Ontario, Canada
Opening hours: Open daily

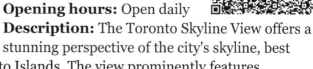

Description: The Toronto Skyline View offers a stunning perspective of the city's skyline, best appreciated from Toronto Islands. The view prominently features landmarks such as the CN Tower and the Rogers Centre, providing a picturesque contrast against the urban backdrop. To reach this viewpoint, take the ferry from Jack Layton Ferry Terminal to the islands. It is highly recommended to take a water taxi for the return trip during peak times to avoid long waits for the ferry, which costs approximately CAD 40. The view is particularly striking at sunset and night, making it a popular spot for both daytime and evening visits. The Toronto Islands also provide an excellent setting for a relaxing stroll or a leisurely picnic. Nearby attractions include Billy Bishop Airport, where visitors can watch planes land and take off against the skyline.

Nearby Attractions:
- CN Tower
- Rogers Centre
- Billy Bishop Airport

Important Information for Visitors:
- Ferry cost: CAD 9 (about USD 6.70)
- Water taxi cost: CAD 40 (about USD 30)
- Expect large crowds during weekends and peak hours.
- Bring a camera for excellent photo opportunities of the skyline and surrounding areas.

The Haunted Walk of Toronto
Location: 11 Gristmill Lane, Toronto, ON M5A 3C4, Canada
Located in: The Distillery Historic District
Plus Code: JJXQ+WC Toronto, Ontario, Canada
Contact: +1 416-238-1473
Website: www.hauntedwalk.com

Opening Hours:
Monday to Sunday: 10 am – 10 pm

Description:
The Haunted Walk of Toronto offers an engaging tour of the city's spookiest and most mysterious locations. Located in the historic Distillery District, this tour delves into Toronto's eerie past, blending historical facts with ghostly legends. The tour guides, known for their enthusiasm and depth of knowledge, lead visitors through intriguing stories and sites, including lesser-known corners of the city that hold a spooky charm. The experience provides a mix of historical insight and paranormal intrigue, making it a unique way to explore Toronto's darker side.

Nearby attractions include the Distillery Historic District itself, known for its well-preserved Victorian architecture and vibrant arts scene. The area is also home to various shops, galleries, and restaurants, enhancing the overall visit.

Important Information for Visitors:
It is highly recommended to book your tour in advance as spots can fill up quickly. The tours typically run for about 90 minutes and offer a chance to explore the Distillery District in a different light. Dress appropriately for the weather and wear comfortable walking shoes.

Simcoe Park
Location: 255 Wellington St W, Toronto, ON M5V 3G5, Canada
Plus Code: JJV7+W6 Toronto, Ontario, Canada
Contact: +1 416-338-4386
Website: www.toronto.ca
Opening Hours: Open 24 hours
Description: Simcoe Park is a tranquil green space situated in the heart of Toronto, directly across from the Metro Toronto Convention Centre. The park features notable art installations, including a dramatic mountain sculpture and a solemn workers' memorial honoring those who lost their lives at work. It is conveniently located near several landmarks such as the CBC Broadcasting Centre and the Ritz-Carlton Hotel. Visitors can access the underground PATH from the park, which offers a connection to various shops and dining options. The park is a pleasant spot for a stroll or relaxation and is well-positioned for those exploring the nearby attractions.

Nearby Attractions:
- **Metro Toronto Convention Centre**: A major conference and events venue.
- **CBC Broadcasting Centre**: The headquarters for the Canadian Broadcasting Corporation.
- **Ritz-Carlton Hotel**: A luxury hotel providing upscale accommodations.

Important Information for Visitors:
Restrooms are available in the food court located underneath the park, open from 6 am to 9 pm most days. The park is open 24 hours, providing flexibility for visits at any time.

Half House
Location: 54 St Patrick St, Toronto, ON M5T 1V1, Canada
Plus Code: MJ26+Q6 Toronto, Ontario, Canada
Opening Hours: Open 24 hours
Description:
Half House is a unique architectural curiosity in Toronto, notable for its distinctive design where only half of a traditional house is constructed. Located on St Patrick Street, this quirky building stands out among the surrounding modern skyscrapers. Visitors can view the house from the outside; it does not offer interior tours or detailed historical information. The building is a quick stop and is best appreciated as part of a broader exploration of the area. Nearby, Queen Street West offers a variety of shops and dining options for those looking to

continue their outing.
Nearby Attractions:
- **Queen Street West:** A vibrant shopping and dining district located just a block away.

Important Information for Visitors:
Parking can be challenging, and since the attraction is visible only from the outside, it is recommended to combine your visit with other nearby activities.

Rodney The Tree
Location: 44 Massey St, Toronto, ON M6J 2T4, Canada
Plus Code: JHVP+8J Toronto, Ontario, Canada
Opening Hours: Open 24 hours
Description:
Rodney The Tree is a distinctive and beloved natural landmark in Toronto, known for its charming presence in the local community. Located at 44 Massey Street,

this tree has garnered a reputation for its unique character and the sense of serenity it provides. It stands as a notable feature in the area, especially appreciated by those who value a quiet moment in nature amidst the urban environment. Rodney The Tree is located near Trinity Bellwoods Park, making it a convenient stop for visitors exploring the park or the surrounding neighborhood. While there is no formal infrastructure or historical information available at the site, the tree's presence alone offers a peaceful retreat from the city hustle.

Nearby Attractions:
- **Trinity Bellwoods Park:** A large, popular park offering green space and recreational facilities, located adjacent to Rodney The Tree.

Important Information for Visitors:
The tree is accessible at any time of day, and no reservation is required. It is recommended to visit while exploring the nearby park or if seeking a quiet outdoor experience. Parking is available in the vicinity, but can be limited during busy times.

Big Heart
Location: 24 Tank House Lane, Toronto, ON M5A 3C4, Canada
Plus Code: MJ2Q+27 Toronto, Ontario, Canada
Opening Hours: Open 24 hours
Description: Big Heart is a popular and visually striking attraction located in the Distillery Historic District of Toronto. This large heart-shaped sculpture serves as a charming photo opportunity and a symbol of affection and community. Positioned in a vibrant area known for its historic architecture and artistic ambiance, the Big Heart attracts both locals and visitors, especially couples and tourists. While it is a prominent feature for photo enthusiasts, it can experience high foot traffic, particularly during peak times like weekends and public holidays. For those interested in exploring further, the

Distillery District offers a variety of artisan shops, cafes, and other attractions, including the LOVE lock installation, which can also be a notable stop.

Nearby Attractions:

- **The Distillery Historic District:** A historic area known for its cobblestone streets, art galleries, boutiques, and restaurants. It features numerous attractions and landmarks within walking distance.

Important Information for Visitors:

The attraction is accessible around the clock and does not require a reservation. It is advisable to visit during off-peak hours to avoid long wait times for photos. The surrounding Distillery District offers a range of activities and amenities, making it a worthwhile area to explore in conjunction with a visit to Big Heart.

City Sightseeing Toronto
Location: 1 Dundas St E, Toronto, ON M5B, Canada
Plus Code: MJ49+GW Toronto, Ontario, Canada
Contact: +1 416-410-0536
Website:
citysightseeingtoronto.com
Opening Hours:
Monday to Friday: 9 am – 5 pm
Saturday to Sunday: 9 am – 5 pm
Closed on: Public Holidays
Description:
City Sightseeing Toronto offers a "Hop On Hop Off" bus service that provides a convenient way to explore the city. Operating from Dundas Station, the service includes a double-decker bus tour and an optional harbor and island cruise. Tickets, which can be purchased online or offline, are valid for 24 hours from the time of purchase. The tour features knowledgeable guides who provide live commentary, enhancing the sightseeing experience. The service allows flexibility to hop on and off at various stops, providing a comprehensive view of Toronto's key attractions. Additionally, discounted tickets for popular sights like the CN Tower and Casa Loma can be bought on the bus.

Nearby Attractions:
- **Harbor and Island Cruise:** Enjoy a scenic boat ride to explore Toronto's waterfront and islands.
- **CN Tower:** A must-see iconic landmark offering panoramic views of the city.
- **Casa Loma:** A historic castle with beautiful gardens and intriguing architecture.

Important Information for Visitors:

The bus service is popular among tourists and can get busy, especially during peak times. While the service provides flexibility and a broad overview of the city, some visitors have noted issues with bus frequency and the clarity of commentary. It is advisable to check the schedule and plan for possible delays. Pre-purchasing tickets and exploring additional attractions on the route can enhance the experience.

Black Creek Pioneer Village
Location: 1000 Murray Ross Pkwy, Toronto, ON M3J 2P3, Canada
Plus Code: QFFM+96 Toronto, Ontario, Canada
Contact: +1 416-736-1733
Website:  blackcreek.ca
Opening Hours:
Wednesday to Thursday: 11 am – 4 pm
Friday to Sunday: 11 am – 4 pm
Description:
Black Creek Pioneer Village is an interactive historical site that offers a glimpse into 19th-century life in Ontario. The village features a collection of historic buildings, including homes, a schoolhouse, and a church, many of which have been relocated from various locations around the province. Visitors can explore these buildings and participate in demonstrations led by costumed staff who provide insights into traditional crafts and daily activities from the pioneer era. The village is well-maintained and provides a relaxed, educational experience suitable for families and history enthusiasts alike. Popular activities include observing printing demonstrations and enjoying freshly baked goods from the inn. The site

has limited food offerings, so visitors are encouraged to bring their own meals or visit nearby dining options. To maximize the visit, it is advisable to spend at least a few hours exploring the village and its interactive exhibits.

Nearby Attractions:

- **Toronto Zoo:** Explore a diverse collection of animals and conservation efforts.
- **Royal Ontario Museum:** Discover extensive exhibits on natural history, art, and culture.
- **York University:** Located nearby, offering cultural and educational events.

Important Information for Visitors:

- The village is open on weekends and select weekdays; it is closed on Mondays and Tuesdays.
- Tickets can be purchased at the entrance or online, with discounts available for online purchases.
- Wear comfortable walking shoes and bring water, as there is moderate walking involved.

Bobbie Rosenfeld Park
Location: 294 Bremner Blvd, Toronto, ON M5V 3L9, Canada
Plus Code: JJR7+M4 Toronto, Ontario, Canada
Contact: +1 416-392-2489
Website: toronto.ca
Opening Hours: Open 24 hours
Description:
Bobbie Rosenfeld Park is a small, open green space situated near major Toronto landmarks such as the CN Tower and Rogers Centre. This park offers a brief respite in a bustling area, with seating available for visitors to relax and enjoy the surrounding city views. It features a small pond, though the water feature may not always be operational. While the park provides a shaded area, it may not always be well-maintained, with occasional issues such as fallen tiles or litter. Despite these concerns, it serves as a convenient spot to rest before or after visiting nearby attractions. It is recommended to visit if you are in the

area, particularly if you are seeking a quiet moment amidst the city's activity.

Nearby Attractions:
- **CN Tower:** A major landmark offering panoramic views of Toronto from its observation deck.
- **Rogers Centre:** A multi-purpose stadium known for hosting major sporting events and concerts.
- **Ripley's Aquarium of Canada:** Features an extensive collection of marine life and interactive exhibits.

Important Information for Visitors:
- There are no restrooms or playground facilities within the park.
- The park's pond may not always have water, and maintenance issues can occasionally impact the park's appearance.

Olympic Park
Location: 222 Bremner Blvd, Toronto, ON M5V 2T6, Canada
Plus Code: JJV8+35 Toronto, Ontario, Canada
Website: toronto.ca
Opening Hours: Open 24 hours
Description:

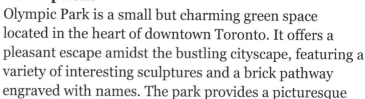

Olympic Park is a small but charming green space located in the heart of downtown Toronto. It offers a pleasant escape amidst the bustling cityscape, featuring a variety of interesting sculptures and a brick pathway engraved with names. The park provides a picturesque view of the nearby CN Tower and is situated near major attractions like the Metro Toronto Convention Centre, Rogers Centre, and Ripley's Aquarium. While the park is relatively small, it is valued for its landscaping and the opportunity it provides for a restful break. The area includes benches and well-maintained flowers and trees, although some visitors have noted that the park's upkeep can vary. It's a suitable spot for a quick visit, relaxing, or taking photos of the surrounding landmarks.

Nearby Attractions:
- **CN Tower:** Offers stunning views from its observation deck.
- **Rogers Centre:** Multi-purpose stadium for sports and concerts.
- **Ripley's Aquarium of Canada:** Features marine life exhibits.

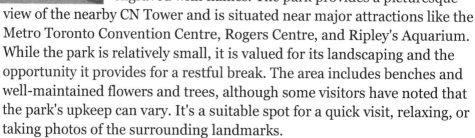

- **Metro Toronto Convention Centre:** Hosts various events and conventions.

Important Information for Visitors:
- The park is dog-friendly.
- Facilities are limited to benches and basic landscaping.
- Maintenance may vary, with some visitors noting the park's condition can sometimes be less than ideal.

TRAVEL

DATE:

DURATION:

DESTINATION:

PLACES TO SEE:

1 _____
2 _____
3 _____
4 _____
5 _____
6 _____
7 _____

LOCAL FOOD TO TRY:

1 _____
2 _____
3 _____
4 _____
5 _____
6 _____
7 _____

NOTES

EXPENSES IN TOTAL:

JOURNAL

Tommy Thompson Light Beacon Station
Location: Toronto, ON, Canada
Plus Code: JM74+CJ Toronto, Ontario, Canada
Website: toronto.ca
Opening Hours: Open 24 hours

Description: Tommy Thompson Light Beacon Station, located at the end of Tommy Thompson Park, is a scenic and relatively secluded spot offering stunning views of Lake Ontario and the Toronto skyline. The area is perfect for those looking to escape the hustle and bustle of the city and enjoy nature.

The station is accessible via a long, 5km trail that runs through Tommy Thompson Park. The trail is popular for biking and hiking, providing a mix of asphalt and grassy paths. Along the route, you'll encounter unique sculptures made from construction materials and can enjoy a peaceful environment with minimal crowds, especially on weekday evenings. The lighthouse itself, positioned at the end of the park, provides panoramic views of the lake and city. The climb to the top involves navigating two ladders, which might be challenging for those with vertigo or a fear of heights. However, the effort is rewarded with breathtaking vistas, especially at sunset.

Key Features:
- Scenic bike and hiking trails
- Unique construction garbage sculptures
- Panoramic views of Toronto and Lake Ontario
- Quiet and less crowded, ideal for meditation and relaxation

Important Information for Visitors:
- The park is a 6km demi-island with a mix of paved and grassy trails.
- Mosquitoes can be an issue in the evenings, so consider bringing repellent.
- The climb to the top of the lighthouse can be strenuous and is not suitable for everyone.

Toronto Railway Museum
Location: 255 Bremner Blvd, Toronto, ON M5V 3M9, Canada
Located in: Roundhouse Park
Plus Code: JJR7+7J Toronto, Ontario, Canada
Website: torontorailwaymuseum.com
Opening Hours:
- **Friday:** 12–5 pm
- **Saturday:** 12–5 pm
- **Sunday:** 12–5 pm
- **Monday:** Closed
- **Tuesday:** Closed
- **Wednesday:** 12–5 pm
- **Thursday:** 12–5 pm

Description: The Toronto Railway Museum provides an engaging experience for families, train enthusiasts, and history buffs. Located in Roundhouse Park, the museum features a range of historical locomotives and rolling stock.

Key Attractions:
- **Outdoor Area:** Free access to a diverse collection of historic locomotives and rolling stock.
- **Indoor Area:** Paid admission includes interactive exhibits, a train simulator, and a small collection of model trains.
- **Vintage Passenger Car:** Explore a restored passenger car, though some areas may be closed off.
- **Mini Train Ride:** Available for a separate fee, offering a fun experience for kids.

Nearby Attractions:
- Steam Whistle Brewery
- Ripley's Aquarium
- CN Tower
- Rogers Centre
- The Rec Room

Visitor Tips:
- The outdoor area is accessible without admission, while the indoor section requires a ticket.

- The museum's admission price may feel high relative to the small size of the indoor exhibits.
- Tickets for the mini train ride are sold separately, and there can be a wait for ticket sales.
- The museum can be crowded on weekends, and staff enthusiasm may vary.

Toronto Old City Hall
Location: 60 Queen St W, Toronto, ON M5H 2M3, Canada
Plus Code: MJ39+28 Toronto, Ontario, Canada
Opening Hours:

- **Friday:** 8:30 am–4:30 pm
- **Saturday:** Closed
- **Sunday:** Closed
- **Monday:** 8:30 am–4:30 pm
- **Tuesday:** 8:30 am–4:30 pm
- **Wednesday:** 8:30 am–4:30 pm
- **Thursday:** 8:30 am–4:30 pm

Description: Toronto Old City Hall, completed in 1899, is a striking example of Romanesque architecture with a prominent clock tower. Originally used as the city's municipal headquarters, it now operates as a courthouse.

Key Attractions:
- **Architectural Design:** The building features elaborate Romanesque details, including animal and human carvings, a grand clock tower, and a stunning interior with mosaic floors and stained glass windows.
- **Historical Significance:** Served as Toronto's city hall until 1966 and continues to be a major courthouse in Canada.
- **Public Access:** Visitors can enter the building for minor traffic offences and observe its historic and architectural beauty.

Visitor Tips:
- **Security Procedures:** Expect strict security when entering, as the building functions as a courthouse.
- **Photogenic Spot:** The exterior and interior of the building are excellent for photography.

- **Nearby Attractions:** Located near Nathan Phillips Square, where the iconic Toronto sign is situated, and a great stop while exploring downtown.

Ideal For: Architecture enthusiasts, history buffs, and anyone interested in Toronto's cultural heritage.

Queen's Quay Terminal
Location: 207 Queens Quay W Suite 141, Toronto, ON M5J 1A7, Canada
Plus Code: JJQ9+HP Toronto, Ontario, Canada
Opening Hours: 9 am–5 pm
Description: Queen's Quay Terminal is a historic waterfront building that blends old-world charm with modern amenities. It serves as a hub for shopping, dining, and cultural experiences.

Key Attractions:
- **Shops and Restaurants:** Features a variety of boutique shops and upscale dining options.
- **Cultural Attractions:** Hosts art galleries and cultural exhibitions.
- **Views:** Offers stunning views of Lake Ontario and the Toronto skyline from its iconic clock tower.

Visitor Tips:
- **Accessibility:** Be aware that some escalators may not be working; check for alternative elevator access.
- **Crowds:** Can get busy during peak times, and parking might be challenging.
- **Events:** The terminal hosts events and exhibitions, which can enhance the experience.

Ideal For: Those interested in a mix of shopping, dining, and cultural experiences, with a picturesque waterfront setting.

Gooderham Building

Location: 49 Wellington St E, Toronto, ON M5E 1C9, Canada

Plus Code: JJXG+97 Toronto, Ontario, Canada

Description: The Gooderham Building, often referred to as the "Flatiron Building," was constructed in 1892 and designed by David Roberts Jr. It is famous for its distinctive wedge shape, making it a notable architectural landmark in Toronto. The building predates the more famous Flatiron Building in New York by about a decade.

Key Features:
- **Architectural Style:** Recognizable for its unique flatiron shape, reminiscent of architectural styles found in the UK.
- **Historic Significance:** A prime example of 19th-century architecture, and one of Toronto's most iconic buildings.
- **Surroundings:** Located near a dog fountain park and offers great photo opportunities with its vintage look and interesting backdrop.

Visitor Tips:
- **Parking:** Paid parking is available on the side of the road.
- **Photography:** The building provides excellent photo opportunities, especially with its unique design and the surrounding historic architecture.

Ontario Place

Location: 955 Lake Shore Blvd W, Toronto, ON M6K 3B9, Canada

Plus Code: JHHJ+CP Toronto, Ontario, Canada

Description: Ontario Place is a waterfront cultural, leisure, and entertainment park located in downtown Toronto. While the site is currently undergoing redevelopment, it remains a popular destination for walking, scenic views, and outdoor events such as concerts and the annual air show.

Key Features:

- **Concert Venue:** Ontario Place is known for its concert venues, though patrons should be aware that some seating areas are not covered and may have obstructed views.
- **Walking Trails:** The waterfront trails offer stunning views, making it a great spot for a refreshing walk by the water.
- **Picnic Areas:** Ample grassy areas are available for picnicking, with some shaded spots perfect for a relaxing day outdoors.

Facilities:

- **Restrooms:** Restrooms are available, but the quality varies depending on the crowds and events.
- **Food and Drinks:** A variety of food and drink options are available, but prices tend to be high.

Visitor Tips:

- **Parking:** Parking can be an issue due to ongoing construction. It's recommended to take public transit or park at nearby locations such as CNE, especially for those with disabilities.
- **Plan Ahead:** Due to the redevelopment, some areas may be closed, but the venue still offers great experiences for visitors seeking a connection with nature or attending concerts.

Ideal For: Concertgoers, families, and those looking for a scenic waterfront walk or a relaxed outdoor picnic.

The Little House

Location: 128 Day Ave, Toronto, ON M6E 3W2, Canada

Plus Code: MHM2+MQ Toronto, Ontario, Canada

Description: The Little House is an iconic, quirky feature in Toronto, known for being the smallest house in the city. At just 300 square feet, it sits inconspicuously on a "normal" residential street, situated between larger, more traditional homes. Despite its tiny size, this house has become a point of curiosity and intrigue for both locals and visitors.

Key Features:
- **Unique Attraction:** The Little House is an architectural novelty that stands out for its miniature size. It's a great quick stop for those exploring unique Toronto landmarks.
- **Famous Spot:** The house gained international recognition after being featured on "The Ellen DeGeneres Show," adding to its fame.
- **Residential:** Although it's a tourist curiosity, the house is still a functioning home.

Visitor Tips:
- **Drive-By Visit:** Many visitors prefer to do a quick drive-by to see The Little House, as there isn't much to explore inside unless you're familiar with the owner.
- **Great Photo Op:** It's a popular spot for photos due to its charming and unconventional design.

Ideal For: Architecture lovers, curious travelers, and anyone looking for a fun and quick stop in Toronto to see a unique part of the city's charm

TRAVEL

DATE:

DURATION:

DESTINATION:

PLACES TO SEE:	LOCAL FOOD TO TRY:

PLACES TO SEE:

1 _____
2 _____
3 _____
4 _____
5 _____
6 _____
7 _____

LOCAL FOOD TO TRY:

1 _____
2 _____
3 _____
4 _____
5 _____
6 _____
7 _____

NOTES

EXPENSES IN TOTAL:

JOURNAL

Daydream Adventures

Location: 1803 Danforth Ave, Toronto, ON M4C 1J2, Canada

Plus code: MMMJ+PG Toronto, Ontario, Canada

Contact: +1 437-245-4535

Website: www.daydreamtoronto.com

Opening hours:

Monday to Thursday: 12pm – 11pm

Friday: 11am – 12am

Saturday and Sunday: 10am – 12am

Description:

Daydream Adventures offers an immersive escape room experience in Toronto. Located on Danforth Avenue, it features intricately designed rooms with handcrafted props and interactive puzzles. Visitors can choose from themed rooms like the "Ice Cave" or the "Mystical Forest," each offering a unique and engaging challenge. The escape rooms are designed for both seasoned players and newcomers, with the puzzles offering variety beyond traditional lock-and-key systems. The attraction is located in a basement, so accessibility may be an issue for those with mobility challenges. The staff is known for being friendly and accommodating, enhancing the overall experience. Daydream Adventures is family-friendly, and it is highly recommended to book in advance for a seamless visit.

Nearby Attractions:

Located along Danforth Avenue, visitors have easy access to nearby local shops and eateries, perfect for exploring before or after the adventure.

Important Information for Visitors:

Due to its basement location, Daydream Adventures may not be accessible for everyone. There is no air conditioning, so it's advisable to dress lightly. Parking might be limited in the area, and public transportation is a recommended option.

Toronto's Art Escape Room

Location: 383 King St W, Toronto, ON M5V 1K1, Canada

Plus code: JJW4+7J Toronto, Ontario, Canada

Contact: +1 647-417-1122

Website: www.escapemanor.com

Opening hours:

Monday: Closed

Tuesday to Thursday: 4pm – 12am

Friday and Saturday: 11am – 1am

Sunday: 11am – 12am

Description:

Toronto's Art Escape Room, also known as Escape Manor, offers a multifaceted experience in the heart of the city. Located on King Street West, this unique attraction combines escape rooms, axe throwing, board games, and a lounge. Each escape room is meticulously designed with immersive themes such as "Cabin 13" and "Devil's Advocate," delivering both challenging puzzles and captivating storytelling. The basement features escape rooms, while the top floor is dedicated to axe throwing. Drinks and food are available throughout, including inside the escape rooms. The venue is known for its vibrant atmosphere, with friendly staff who enhance the experience with engaging role-play. Board games and lounge spaces allow visitors to relax before or after their escape adventures.

Nearby Attractions:

Located in the entertainment district, Toronto's Art Escape Room is close to attractions like the CN Tower, Ripley's Aquarium of Canada, and the Rogers Centre, making it a convenient stop for tourists exploring the area.

Important Information for Visitors:

It is highly recommended to arrive 10 minutes early to complete necessary waivers. Public transportation is advisable due to heavy traffic in the area.

Tai Pan Tours
Location: 3621 Hwy 7 Suite 509, Markham, ON L3R 0G6, Canada
Located in: Liberty Square
Plus code: VM37+J4 Markham, Ontario, Canada
Contact: +1 416-646-8828
Website: www.taipantours.com
Opening hours:
Monday to Friday: 10am – 6:30pm
Saturday: 11am – 4:30pm
Sunday: Closed

Description: Tai Pan Tours is a well-regarded tour company based in Markham, Ontario, offering expertly guided tours across various regions in Eastern Canada. The company is recognized for its comprehensive tour packages, such as the popular three-day trip to Ottawa, Montreal, and Quebec City, as well as the seven-day Eastern Canada Prince Edward Island and Maritimes Tour. Each tour is carefully organized, providing visitors with comfortable accommodations, reliable transport, and a structured itinerary that includes scenic views and places of historical significance. The tour guides are knowledgeable, fluent in multiple languages including English, Mandarin, and Cantonese, and are known for their friendly demeanor and professionalism. Tours feature stops at key Canadian landmarks, ensuring visitors get a well-rounded experience of the country's culture and history. Whether exploring the vibrant cities of Quebec or delving into the picturesque landscapes of Prince Edward Island, Tai Pan Tours ensures a memorable and enriching experience. It is recommended to book in advance due to the popularity of these tours.

Nearby Attractions:
Liberty Square is located near various shopping centers and dining options in Markham. The Toronto Zoo and Pacific Mall are also within a reasonable driving distance for visitors interested in extending their stay.

Important Information for Visitors:
Booking ahead is essential, especially during peak travel seasons. The tours generally operate on tight schedules, so punctuality is highly recommended.

Little Canada

Location: 10 Dundas St E Basement2, Toronto, ON M5B 2G9, Canada

Located in: The Tenor

Plus code: MJ49+MM Toronto, Ontario, Canada

Contact: +1 647-578-4663

Website: www.little-canada.ca

Opening hours:

Monday to Sunday: 10am – 7:30pm

Description: Little Canada is a delightful miniature world located in downtown Toronto that offers visitors a captivating glimpse into Canada's most iconic landmarks and landscapes. The attraction showcases an intricately crafted and highly detailed model of Canada, featuring cities, towns, and natural wonders from across the country. Walking through Little Canada feels like embarking on a miniature journey across Canada, from the urban skyline of Toronto to the majestic Rockies. The attention to detail in each exhibit is remarkable, with sound, lighting, and moving effects bringing the scenes to life. Little Canada is an engaging experience for both adults and children, with interactive games such as a moose hunt, and opportunities to talk to the model makers as they continue to expand the displays. It is highly recommended for locals and tourists alike, providing a unique and enjoyable way to experience the vast diversity of Canada all in one place.

Nearby Attractions:

Little Canada is conveniently located near Yonge-Dundas Square, the CF Toronto Eaton Centre, and the Art Gallery of Ontario, all within walking distance in downtown Toronto.

Important Information for Visitors:

Little Canada is family-friendly and accessible to all ages. Due to its central location, taking public transportation or parking in nearby lots is recommended for ease of access

Fantasy Fair
Location: 500 Rexdale Blvd Unit F006, Etobicoke, ON M9W 6K5, Canada
Located in: Woodbine Mall & Fantasy Fair
Plus code: PCC2+26 Etobicoke, Ontario, Canada
Contact: +1 437-880-8448
Website: fantasyfair.ca
Opening hours:
Monday to Sunday: 11am – 7pm
Description: Fantasy Fair is an indoor amusement park located within the Woodbine Mall in Etobicoke, offering a variety of rides, activities, and attractions for children and families. Although the park has seen better days, it remains a fun place for younger kids with its rides, indoor playground, bumper cars, arcade games, and even dinosaur displays. For older kids, there's rock climbing and additional activities. Visitors have noted that some of the rides may be outdated or out of order, and the park lacks air conditioning during hot summer days, which could be an issue for comfort. However, it remains a nostalgic venue with friendly staff, providing an affordable and convenient entertainment option for families in the area.

Key Features:
- Indoor playground with large slides
- Carousel, bumper cars, and other fun rides
- Rock climbing and arcade games for older children
- Dinosaur-themed displays
- Family-friendly environment

Nearby Attractions:
The park is located within Woodbine Mall, offering shopping and additional entertainment options. Visitors may also want to explore the nearby racetrack and casino for additional activities.

Visitor Tips:
- Day passes are priced around $27, making it an affordable option for families.
- Groupons and discounts may be available, especially on weekdays.

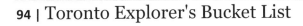

- Given some outdated facilities and potential closures of certain rides, it is advisable to check the operational status of attractions before purchasing tickets.
- As there is no air conditioning, dressing lightly in the summer is recommended.
- The park can be quiet on weekdays, which may result in less waiting but also fewer rides operating.

Important Notes:
Some visitors have expressed dissatisfaction with the park's maintenance, cleanliness, and overall upkeep. While still a fun option for children, the park could benefit from updates and revitalization.

LEGOLAND Discovery Centre Toronto
Location: 1 Bass Pro Mills Dr, Vaughan, ON L4K 5W4, Canada
Located in: Vaughan Mills
Plus code: RFF7+XR Vaughan, Ontario, Canada
Contact: +1 905-761-7066
Website: legolanddiscoverycentre.ca
Opening hours:
- Monday to Saturday: 10 am – 6 pm
- Sunday: 11 am – 6 pm

Description: LEGOLAND Discovery Centre Toronto is an indoor Lego-themed attraction located within Vaughan Mills, offering a variety of interactive Lego experiences for children and families. The center includes several zones where visitors can explore Lego exhibits, build and test their own creations, enjoy rides, watch 4D movies, and experience hands-on fun. Highlights include impressive Lego models of landmarks, characters, and vehicles, as well as a 4D cinema that adds an extra dimension of excitement to the visit. There's also a VR experience for an immersive adventure.

Key Features:
- **Rides:** Enjoy Lego-themed rides, including a Kingdom Quest adventure.
- **4D Cinema:** Experience a movie with 3D visuals and added special effects like mist and wind.

- **Build and Play Zones:** Explore themed areas where you can construct and test your Lego creations.
- **Lego Miniland:** View intricate models of famous landmarks, all made out of Lego bricks.
- **VR Experience:** A thrilling virtual reality ride for an extra fee.
- **Café and Lego Store:** Take a break and grab a snack, or shop for your favorite Lego sets to take home.

Visitor Tips:
- **Crowds:** The center can get busy, especially during weekends and holidays. Visiting during off-peak hours can provide a more relaxed experience.
- **4D Cinema:** Highly recommended for visitors of all ages. Be prepared for some mist effects during the show.
- **Online Booking:** Purchase tickets online to save money, especially if you're planning on adding extras like the VR experience.
- **Duration:** Plan for around 2-3 hours to explore everything.
- **Kid-Focused:** While the activities are primarily aimed at children, adults can also enjoy the creativity and fun atmosphere.

Nearby Attractions:
Vaughan Mills offers shopping and dining options, making it a convenient stop for a day of fun and exploration. Additionally, other attractions in the area include the nearby Reptilia Zoo and Canada's Wonderland.

Important Notes:
Some exhibits and features might be in need of maintenance, but the friendly and enthusiastic staff enhance the overall experience. For families with young children, LEGOLAND Discovery Centre Toronto is a playful and creative day out, with plenty of opportunities to engage in imaginative activities and build lasting memories.

Chester Hill Lookout
Location: Chester Hill Rd, Toronto, ON M4K 1V4, Canada
Plus code: MJJQ+F7 Toronto, Ontario, Canada
Opening hours: Open 24 hours

Description:
Chester Hill Lookout is a hidden gem in Toronto that offers a picturesque view of the city's skyline, the Don Valley Parkway (DVP), and the Evergreen Brickworks. It's a popular spot for photographers, especially at night when long exposure shots capture the busy highway and city lights. This lookout provides a peaceful place to relax, enjoy the sunset, or catch the beauty of the Toronto skyline from a unique angle.

Visitor Notes:

- **Overgrown Vegetation:** As of July 2024, some vegetation is blocking parts of the view, but there is still a small open area where the downtown skyline is visible.
- **Astrology Painting:** Recently repainted, adding a nice artistic touch to the area.
- **Residential Area:** Best accessed by public transportation (Broadview station nearby) or on foot, as parking is limited and mostly residential.
- **Photography Spot:** Ideal for evening or night photography, offering stunning views of the city lights and highway traffic.
- **Quiet Environment:** The lookout is in a quiet neighborhood, so visitors are encouraged to be respectful, avoid loud noise, and keep the area clean.
- **No Facilities:** There are no public washrooms or other amenities nearby.

Nearby Attractions:
Close to Riverdale Park, which offers similar views from a different perspective. Evergreen Brickworks is also nearby for those interested in nature trails and eco-friendly spaces.

The Yorkville Rock
Location: 131 Cumberland St, Toronto, ON M5S 2W7, Canada
Plus code: MJ95+X4 Toronto, Ontario, Canada
Located in: Village of Yorkville Park
Opening hours: Open 24 hours
Description:
The Yorkville Rock is a remarkable geological feature

located in the Village of Yorkville Park, Toronto. This large glacial rock, believed to be approximately a billion years old, was transported from the Canadian Shield. It sits in the heart of Yorkville, offering a unique contrast to the urban surroundings and serving as a historical reminder of Canada's ancient landscape.

Visitor Experience:

- **Natural Wonder:** The Yorkville Rock is a fascinating sight, featuring a crater-like structure formed from different types of rock fused together. Visitors often find themselves admiring its size and rugged beauty.
- **Great for Photos:** The rock is a popular spot for photos, especially for families with children who enjoy climbing it in the summer.
- **Seating Area:** Visitors can relax around the rock, sit on nearby benches or tables, and enjoy the lively Yorkville atmosphere.
- **Events:** The Yorkville Rock sometimes hosts events like the Jazz Festival or live performances, adding to the vibrant culture of the area.
- **Urban Oasis:** Though not necessarily peaceful due to its central location, it offers a place to unwind, people-watch, or simply enjoy a coffee from nearby cafes.

Nearby Attractions:

The Yorkville area is known for its luxury shopping, cafes, and dining. Visitors can explore the trendy neighborhood, visit nearby art galleries, or simply take in the blend of natural beauty and urban charm that Yorkville offers.

Churchill Memorial
Location: Toronto, ON M5G 1R1, Canada
Plus code: MJ38+C2 Toronto, Ontario, Canada
Located near: Nathan Phillips Square, Northwest side of City Hall, near the corner of Armoury and Chestnut Streets
Opening Hours: Open 24 hours
Description: The Churchill Memorial in Toronto is a bronze statue dedicated to Sir Winston Churchill, a key figure in World War II. Originally dedicated in 1977 by then-

Mayor David Crombie, the statue was commissioned by the late Henry R. Jackman and sculpted by the famous artist Oscar Nemon. Standing 10 feet tall, this statue honors Churchill's leadership during a time of global conflict and the role he played in ensuring the preservation of democratic values.

Visitor Experience:

- **Historical Reflection:** Visitors are invited to reflect on Churchill's complex legacy. As a wartime leader, his contributions to the Allied victory in World War II are undeniable, but his imperialist policies also spark debates, especially in the context of modern discussions about equality, diversity, and inclusion (EDI).
- **Public Space:** The statue is located near benches and within a lively area of Nathan Phillips Square. This makes it a convenient spot to sit, relax, or even have lunch while surrounded by the history of World War II memorials.
- **Controversy:** Some visitors question the appropriateness of celebrating Churchill, given his colonialist actions. This discussion highlights ongoing re-evaluations of historical figures within the context of contemporary values.

Nearby Attractions:

The statue is part of a series of World War II memorials near City Hall. Nathan Phillips Square is a bustling area with nearby cafes, landmarks, and plenty of public seating, making it a popular spot for locals and tourists alike

Gibson House Museum
Location: 5172 Yonge St, Toronto, ON M2N 5P6, Canada
Plus code: QH9P+V2 Toronto, Ontario, Canada

Opening Hours:
- Friday to Sunday: 11 am–5 pm
- Closed on Monday and Tuesday
- Wednesday to Thursday: 11 am–5 pm

Contact:
- Phone: +1 416-395-7432
- Website: toronto.ca

Description: The Gibson House Museum is a preserved historical home located in North York, Toronto, once belonging to David Gibson, a notable public figure of the 19th century. This museum offers a rich glimpse into the life of the Gibson family and the social and political history of Toronto during that period.

The museum's small yet intimate setting features tours guided by knowledgeable staff, such as Ms. Maureen and Sam, who offer fascinating insights into the history of the house and the family that lived there. Guests can explore various exhibits showcasing historical culinary, gardening, farming, and textile arts.

Visitor Experience:

- **Free Admission:** The Gibson House Museum is one of Toronto's ten free admission museums, open from Wednesday to Sunday.
- **Guided Tours:** The staff at the museum are highly praised for their friendliness, professionalism, and in-depth knowledge. The museum offers enriching tours that last around an hour and provide insights into Toronto's history. Ms. Maureen and Sam, in particular, are highlighted for their exceptional storytelling and dedication to creating a welcoming experience.
- **Special Events:** Visitors can sometimes enjoy special art unveilings, hands-on experiences like weaving on a loom, and even sampling gingerbread or cedar tea.
- **Accessibility:** The museum is easy to access via public transit, with a short 10-minute walk from North York Centre Station. Limited free parking is also available.

Notable Highlights:

- The museum provides an immersive experience with various culinary, gardening, and textile arts displays.
- Friendly and devoted staff make the visit memorable, with volunteers always eager to share the history of the Gibson family and their home.
- It's an excellent cultural destination for those interested in Toronto's history and 19th-century life.

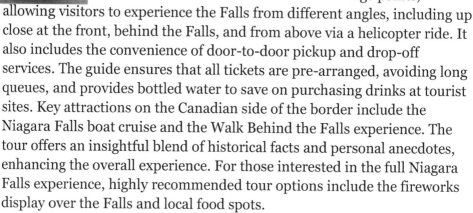

Tour To Niagara Falls

Location: 5400 Robinson St, Niagara Falls, ON L2G 2A6, Canada

Plus code: 3WP9+93 Niagara Falls, Ontario, Canada

Contact: +1 888-786-7906

Website: www.fallstours.ca

Opening hours: Open 24 hours

Description:

This guided tour of Niagara Falls offers an in-depth exploration of one of the world's most famous natural landmarks. The tour covers various vantage points, allowing visitors to experience the Falls from different angles, including up close at the front, behind the Falls, and from above via a helicopter ride. It also includes the convenience of door-to-door pickup and drop-off services. The guide ensures that all tickets are pre-arranged, avoiding long queues, and provides bottled water to save on purchasing drinks at tourist sites. Key attractions on the Canadian side of the border include the Niagara Falls boat cruise and the Walk Behind the Falls experience. The tour offers an insightful blend of historical facts and personal anecdotes, enhancing the overall experience. For those interested in the full Niagara Falls experience, highly recommended tour options include the fireworks display over the Falls and local food spots.

Nearby Attractions:

- Maid of the Mist (American side)
- Niagara Falls Helicopter Ride
- Walk Behind the Falls

Important Information for Visitors:

It is recommended to book the tour in advance to ensure all tickets and attractions are pre-arranged. Visitors should bring suitable clothing for potential mist and rain from the Falls, as well as snacks for longer tours.

Go Tours Canada - Distillery District

Location: 11 Gristmill Lane, Toronto, ON M5A 3C4, Canada

Plus code: JJXQ+WC Toronto, Ontario, Canada

Contact: +1 416-677-3831

Website: www.gotourscanada.com

Opening hours:

Tuesday to Sunday: 11 am – 5 pm

Closed on Monday

Description:

Go Tours Canada offers an engaging and informative way to explore the Distillery District in Toronto, combining history with a unique experience. The tours are conducted on Segways or as walking tours, each offering a fascinating dive into the history of the district, which was once home to the largest distillery in the British Empire. The 30-minute Segway tours provide a fun and different perspective, perfect for both beginners and those experienced with the equipment, while the one-hour walking tours are a more traditional way to explore the area. Guides are knowledgeable and passionate about Toronto's history and are always ready to share interesting anecdotes and answer questions. The tours are designed to be informative, interactive, and entertaining, making them a popular option for both locals and tourists alike. Food and drink options are available in the district, making it a great stop for a full day of exploring.

Nearby Attractions:

- The Distillery Historic District (shops, restaurants, and art galleries)
- Mill Street Brewery
- Toronto Christmas Market (seasonal)

Important Information for Visitors:

Reservations are highly recommended to secure a spot on the tours, especially on weekends. It's advisable to arrive with an appetite as the district offers excellent food and drink options. The tours operate in all weather conditions, so dress accordingly.

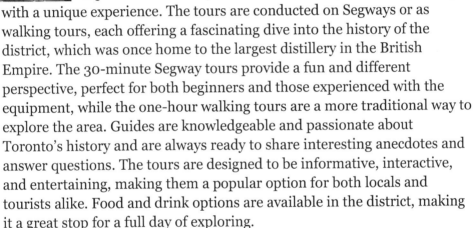

St. Lawrence Market
Location: Toronto, ON M5E 1C3, Canada
Plus code: JJXH+F9 Toronto, Ontario, Canada
Contact: +1 416-392-7219
Website: www.stlawrencemarket.com
Opening hours:
Tuesday to Friday: 9 am – 7 pm
Saturday: 7 am – 5 pm
Sunday: 10 am – 5 pm
Closed on Monday
Description:
St. Lawrence Market is a renowned food destination in Toronto, offering an impressive variety of fresh produce, seafood, meats, cheeses, and baked goods. As one of the city's oldest and most vibrant markets, it attracts locals and tourists alike. The market features numerous specialty shops, such as those offering caviar, fresh coffee beans, and gourmet delicacies. For those looking for a meal, there are plenty of food stalls serving a range of dishes, including sandwiches, pastries, and seafood. Seating is limited indoors, so grabbing food to go and eating outside is recommended during busy times. This market is not just a shopping destination but also a cultural experience, showcasing the rich culinary diversity of Toronto. Its lively atmosphere and high-quality offerings make it a must-visit spot in the city.

Nearby Attractions:
- The Distillery Historic District
- Toronto Harbourfront
- Ripley's Aquarium of Canada
- Sugar Beach

Important Information for Visitors:
Be prepared for crowds, especially on weekends. Seating inside the market can be limited, so consider taking your food to eat elsewhere in the vicinity. This market is a great spot for grocery shopping, particularly for those looking for organic and artisanal items.

Canada's Walk of Fame
Location: 68-66 Simcoe St, Toronto, ON M5J 2H5, Canada
Located in: David Pecaut Square
Plus code: JJW7+V7 Toronto, Ontario, Canada
Contact: +1 416-367-9255

Website: www.canadaswalkoffame.com
Opening hours: Open 24 hours
Description: Canada's Walk of Fame, located in David Pecaut Square in Toronto, honors notable Canadians from various fields, including musicians, actors, athletes, and scientists. It features engraved tiles embedded in the sidewalks, which are easily accessible to visitors at no cost. Though it is often understated compared to Hollywood's Walk of Fame, it represents a celebration of Canadian talent and achievement. Visitors can combine their visit with other nearby attractions, such as a nearby park featuring a unique fountain. However, due to the minimal upkeep of the tiles, the walk is often seen as underwhelming. It's best to view this landmark as a brief stop during a tour of the area, rather than a primary destination.

Nearby Attractions:
- Roy Thomson Hall
- The CN Tower
- Ripley's Aquarium of Canada
- Toronto Harbourfront

Important Information for Visitors:
Expect the walk to be less prominent than other famous landmarks and plan to spend a short amount of time there. Consider visiting nearby sites to enhance your overall experience in the area.

Lower Simcoe Street Underpass Murals
Location: Simcoe St Tunnel, Toronto, ON, Canada
Plus code: JJV8+96 Toronto, Ontario, Canada
Opening hours: Open 24 hours

Description:

The Lower Simcoe Street Underpass Murals in Toronto present a stunning tribute to Indigenous culture and heritage. The east side of the underpass features the *Water Wall*, inspired by the work of Josephine Mandamin, an Anishinaabe grandmother who walked nearly 18,000 kilometers around the Great Lakes to raise awareness about the critical importance of water as a resource. On the west side, the *Elder/Honour Wall* showcases 28 portraits of Indigenous Elders and leaders selected by the local community, celebrating the significant contributions of Indigenous Peoples to Toronto. Both murals offer visitors an emotional and thought-provoking experience, deeply rooted in Indigenous connections to the land and water. Although the street is relatively short, it's worth taking a moment to walk through the underpass and reflect on the powerful imagery. While the murals are an impressive sight for those passing by, they are a unique stop for those exploring the area.

Nearby Attractions:

- The CN Tower
- Ripley's Aquarium of Canada
- Toronto Railway Museum
- Harbourfront Centre

Important Information for Visitors:

The underpass is best appreciated as a brief stop while exploring nearby attractions. It's highly recommended to walk through and experience the art firsthand, whether you are a casual passerby or someone keen on Indigenous history and culture.

TRAVEL

DATE:

DURATION:

DESTINATION:

PLACES TO SEE:

1 _____
2 _____
3 _____
4 _____
5 _____
6 _____
7 _____

LOCAL FOOD TO TRY:

1 _____
2 _____
3 _____
4 _____
5 _____
6 _____
7 _____

NOTES

EXPENSES IN TOTAL:

JOURNAL

The Yorkville Royal Sonesta Hotel Toronto
Location: 220 Bloor St W, Toronto, ON M5S 1T8, Canada
Plus code: MJ93+CC Toronto, Ontario, Canada
Contact: +1 416-960-5200
Website: www.sonesta.com
Check-in time: 16:00
Check-out time: 11:00
Description: The Yorkville Royal Sonesta Hotel Toronto is situated in the heart of Toronto's vibrant Yorkville district, offering convenient access to numerous dining options and cultural attractions. The Royal Ontario Museum and Bata Shoe Museum are directly across the street, while Casa Loma is also nearby. The hotel provides a comfortable stay with clean and spacious rooms, though service is noted for being basic without additional touches. The location offers a lively urban experience with various amenities within walking distance. The hotel is also LGBTQ+ friendly.
Nearby Attractions: Royal Ontario Museum, Bata Shoe Museum, Casa Loma

Ace Hotel Toronto
Location: 51 Camden St, Toronto, ON M5V 1V2, Canada
Plus code: JJW2+MP Toronto, Ontario, Canada
Contact: +1 416-637-1200
Website: www.acehotel.com

Check-in time: 15:00
Check-out time: 12:00
Description: Ace Hotel Toronto offers a stylish and contemporary experience in the heart of Toronto's garment district. The hotel's vibrant atmosphere is enhanced by its rooftop bar, which provides great views and a lively setting. Rooms are equipped with unique features such as turntables, vinyl records, and guitars, ensuring a memorable stay. The hotel prioritizes guest safety with key card access required for the elevators. Located between King and Queen Streets, it is within walking distance of major attractions and dining options, including the nearby Waterworks Food Hall. The hotel's central location and modern amenities contribute to a comfortable and enjoyable stay.
Nearby Attractions: Rogers Centre, Waterworks Food Hall

Hilton Toronto
Location: 145 Richmond St W, Toronto, ON M5H 2L2, Canada
Plus code: JJX7+WQ Toronto, Ontario, Canada
Contact: +1 416-869-3456
Website: www.hilton.com
Check-in time: 16:00
Check-out time: 11:00
Description: Hilton Toronto is centrally located in Toronto, offering convenient access to downtown attractions. The hotel provides a range of services and amenities designed for both business and leisure travelers. Guests can enjoy the luxury of a well-appointed room and benefit from its proximity to local sites. While the property generally offers a high standard of accommodation, recent feedback indicates variability in service quality and guest experience. Despite these concerns, the location remains a key asset, placing visitors near key cultural and commercial destinations.
Nearby Attractions: Close to downtown Toronto's entertainment and dining options.

1 Hotel Toronto

Location: 550 Wellington St W, Toronto, ON M5V 2V4, Canada
Plus code: JHVX+69 Toronto, Ontario, Canada
Contact: +1 416-640-7778
Website: www.1hotels.com
Check-in time: 16:00
Check-out time: 12:00
Description: 1 Hotel Toronto combines luxury with a focus on wellness and sustainability. Guests are greeted by a sophisticated lobby that features ample lounging space and a stylish bar. Harriet's rooftop, a highlight of the hotel, offers exceptional food and beverages with impressive views. The hotel provides a high level of service, ensuring a memorable stay with personalized touches. Rooms are beautifully designed and maintained to a high standard. Located in a vibrant area, the hotel is close to various pubs, bars, and restaurants, and is a short walk from The Well mall. While the hotel excels in many areas, there have been occasional comments about discomfort with room pillows. The hotel's amenities and attentive staff contribute to a top-tier experience.
Nearby Attractions: The Well mall, various pubs and bars, and local dining options

---

Pantages Hotel Downtown Toronto

Location: 200 Victoria St, Toronto, ON M5B 1V8, Canada
Plus code: MJ3C+V9 Toronto, Ontario, Canada
Contact: +1 416-362-1777
Website: www.pantageshotel.com
Check-in time: 15:00
Check-out time: 11:00
Description: Pantages Hotel Downtown Toronto offers a blend of comfort and convenience in a central location. The hotel provides spacious and well-decorated rooms, some with kitchenettes. Guests have noted the efficient service, including prompt responses to requests for kitchenware and other amenities. The hotel's proximity to key locations like the Eaton

Centre and Massey Hall enhances its appeal. While the hotel maintains high standards of cleanliness and service, occasional issues with room amenities have been reported. Overall, it delivers a good value experience with a quiet environment in the heart of downtown.

Nearby Attractions: Eaton Centre, Massey Hall, CN Tower (about a 20-minute walk)

Chelsea Hotel, Toronto
Location: 33 Gerrard St W, Toronto, ON M5G 1Z4, Canada
Plus code: MJ58+9Q Toronto, Ontario, Canada
Contact: +1 416-595-1975
Website: www.chelseatoronto.com
Check-in time: 15:00
Check-out time: 11:00
Description: Chelsea Hotel, Toronto offers a welcoming atmosphere with attentive service and a central location. Guests appreciate the spacious, clean rooms and modern amenities, including a comfortable king-size bed and thoughtful touches. The hotel provides a peaceful environment despite its downtown setting. It features a range of facilities, including an indoor pool and gym. The location is ideal for accessing local attractions, dining, and shopping. However, some guests have reported issues with room amenities and service, such as delays in providing requested items and occasional miscommunications. Overall, the hotel is praised for its value and comfort, with improvements needed in certain areas.

Nearby Attractions: Close to shopping and dining options, and a short distance from major Toronto landmarks

Novotel Toronto Centre
Location: 45 The Esplanade, Toronto, ON M5E 1W2, Canada
Plus code: JJWG+J7 Toronto, Ontario, Canada

Contact: +1 416-367-8900

Website: <u>Novotel Toronto Centre</u>
Check-in time: 15:00
Check-out time: 12:00
Description: Novotel Toronto Centre is a well-regarded hotel known for its spacious and clean rooms, comfortable beds, and modern amenities. Guests appreciate the hotel's location, which is close to major attractions like the CN Tower and Rogers Centre, as well as Union Station. The hotel features a pool, hot tub, and a restaurant. Many visitors praise the friendly and helpful staff, especially in the breakfast area. While some guests have noted issues with room dampness and noise from the street, overall feedback highlights the hotel's convenience, safety, and value.

Nearby Attractions: CN Tower, Rogers Centre, Union Station, various restaurants and bars

Hotel Highlights:
- Great location with easy access to major attractions
- Clean and spacious rooms
- Friendly and professional staff
- Comfortable beds and good amenities
- Pool and hot tub

Notable Issues:
- Some complaints about room dampness
- Minor noise issues from the street
- Occasional issues with room cleaning schedules and television functionality

Cambridge Suites Toronto
Location: 15 Richmond St E, Toronto, ON M5C 1N2, Canada
Plus code: MJ2C+MR Toronto, Ontario, Canada
Contact: +1 416-368-1990
Website: <u>Cambridge Suites Toronto</u>
Check-in time: 00:00
Check-out time: 00:00
Description: Cambridge Suites Toronto is highly praised for its spacious and clean rooms, excellent location, and

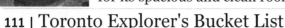

friendly service. It's ideal for families and couples alike, offering comfortable accommodations with convenient amenities. Guests appreciate the central location, which provides easy access to local attractions, restaurants, and public transport. The hotel also offers helpful services, such as early check-in and luggage storage. The inclusion of a kitchenette and ample space in rooms adds to the convenience for longer stays.

Nearby Attractions: Union Station, Rogers Centre, restaurants, convenience stores, public transport

Hotel Highlights:
- Spacious and clean rooms with good amenities
- Friendly and accommodating staff
- Convenient location close to attractions and public transport
- Helpful services like early check-in and luggage storage
- Good value for the price

Notable Features:
- Great view
- Quiet atmosphere
- Good value
- Suitable for families and couples
- Well-equipped rooms with separate living and bathroom areas

Pan Pacific Toronto
Location: 900 York Mills Rd, North York, ON M3B 3H2, Canada
Plus code: QJ4X+PR North York, Ontario, Canada
Contact: +1 416-444-2511
Website: Pan Pacific Toronto
Check-in time: 15:00
Check-out time: 11:00
Description: Pan Pacific Toronto is praised for its elegant design, excellent service, and tranquil setting. The hotel offers spacious and comfortable rooms with stunning views, a well-regarded restaurant, and a variety of amenities including a pool and spa. While the location is somewhat distant from downtown, it is ideal for those needing to be in the North York area with easy access to nearby restaurants and shops.

Nearby Attractions: Various restaurants and coffee shops, midtown attractions

Hotel Highlights:
- Impeccable service
- Spacious, well-designed rooms
- Stunning views
- Excellent on-site restaurant with a great breakfast
- Top-notch amenities, including a pool and spa

Notable Features:
- Quiet location
- Great for business and leisure travelers
- Elegant and inviting lobby
- Some equipment in the fitness center needs maintenance, but other amenities are well-provided

Madison Manor Boutique Hotel
Location: 20 Madison Ave, Toronto, ON M5R 2S1, Canada
Plus code: MH9W+6H Toronto, Ontario, Canada
Contact: +1 416-922-5579
Website: www.madisonmanorboutiquehotel.com
Check-in time: 15:00
Check-out time: 11:00

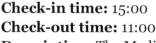

Description: The Madison Manor Boutique Hotel offers a convenient location within a short walking distance of a street filled with restaurants and shops. The hotel features basic amenities, with some rooms providing a quiet retreat from the bustling city. However, guests have reported mixed experiences, including issues with cleanliness and room maintenance. The hotel has a pub on-site, and it is situated near the university, which can contribute to noise levels. The hotel operates under an adult-only policy, requiring all guests to be 19 or older, and does not include breakfast despite previous offerings. It is advisable to check the hotel's policies and room conditions before booking.

Nearby Attractions: The hotel's central location provides easy access to various dining options and shops in the vicinity. Additionally, the proximity to the university may be beneficial for guests attending events or visiting the campus.

The Clarence Park
Location: 7 Clarence Square, Toronto, ON M5V 1H1, Canada
Plus code: JJV4+VC Toronto, Ontario, Canada
Contact: +1 416-591-7387
Website: www.theclarencepark.com
Check-in time: 14:00
Check-out time: 11:00
Description: The Clarence Park offers a budget-friendly accommodation option with a secure and convenient location. It provides complimentary breakfast with options like cereal, oatmeal, and fresh fruit. The property features dorm-style rooms with bunk beds and amenities such as privacy curtains, reading lights, and in-room lockers. While the hostel is praised for its clean and comfortable beds, some shared bathroom facilities are noted as small and lacking in amenities like towels and proper drainage. The hostel is situated in a location that is generally considered safe, though some guests have reported issues with the condition of the rooms and facilities. It is important to review the hostel's policies before booking, as some requirements may not be clearly communicated.
Nearby Attractions: The Clarence Park is located near various restaurants and shops, providing convenient access to local amenities. The area is well-suited for travelers looking for a budget stay with easy access to Toronto's attractions.

Samesun Toronto
Location: 278 Augusta Ave, Toronto, ON M5T 2L9, Canada
Plus code: MH4W+PP Toronto, Ontario, Canada
Contact: +1 416-929-4777

Website: www.samesun.com
Check-in time: 15:00
Check-out time: 11:00
Description: Samesun Toronto offers a vibrant hostel experience with a prime location near Kensington Market and Chinatown. It provides a variety of accommodations including private rooms and dormitories, with features such as comfortable beds, privacy curtains, lockers, and power outlets. The hostel includes clean and well-maintained shared bathrooms and kitchen facilities equipped with essential appliances and utensils. Guests can enjoy a complimentary breakfast and participate in organized social activities like pub crawls and excursions. The property is situated across from bars and restaurants, which adds to its lively atmosphere, though this may contribute to noise levels. The hostel is well-connected to public transport, making it convenient for exploring Toronto.
Nearby Attractions: Samesun Toronto is within walking distance to Kensington Market, CN Tower, and Chinatown, offering easy access to various dining, shopping, and entertainment options.

The Palmerston Toronto
Location: 650 1/2 Queen St W, Toronto, ON M6J 1E4, Canada
Plus code: JHWV+PC Toronto, Ontario, Canada
Contact: +1 416-203-8999
Website: www.secure.webrez.com
Check-in time: 15:00
Check-out time: 11:00
Description: The Palmerston Toronto is a budget accommodation located in the city's Queen Street West area. This hostel-style establishment provides basic amenities and services, but it has faced issues with customer service and management. Guests may encounter challenges with luggage storage policies, as the hostel enforces limits on the amount of luggage allowed in rooms and charges for additional storage. There have been reports of poor communication, overbooking issues, and unavailability of staff. The hostel is situated in a vibrant area, offering easy access to local attractions and dining options.

However, prospective guests should be cautious and ensure they understand the hostel's policies and check recent reviews before booking.

Nearby Attractions: The Palmerston Toronto is well-positioned for exploring Queen Street West and its surrounding areas, known for shopping, dining, and entertainment options.

Filmores Hotel
Location: 212 Dundas St E, Toronto, ON M5A 1Z6, Canada
Plus code: MJ5G+3M Toronto, Ontario, Canada
Contact: +1 416-921-2191
Website: www.filmores.com
Check-in time: 14:00
Check-out time: 11:00
Description: Filmores Hotel offers budget accommodations in a central location in Toronto, adjacent to a strip club. This hotel is known for its basic amenities and is situated in an area with mixed reviews regarding safety and cleanliness. The property provides essential accommodations at an affordable price, with some rooms featuring en-suite bathrooms. However, guests should be aware that the hotel is located in a neighborhood with a reputation for being less desirable and may not be suitable for all travelers. The hotel's proximity to downtown can be a benefit for those on a tight budget.

Nearby Attractions: Located close to downtown Toronto, the hotel provides easy access to various city attractions, although the immediate area may be less appealing.

Comfy Guest House
Location: 250 Gerrard St E, Toronto, ON M5A 2G2, Canada
Plus code: MJ6J+R6 Toronto, Ontario, Canada
Contact: +1 416-822-5590
Website: www.comfyguesthousetoronto.com
Check-in time: 11:45

Check-out time: 11:00

Description: Comfy Guest House is a well-regarded accommodation offering a clean and cozy environment in Toronto. This guest house is known for its comfortable beds, homely atmosphere, and excellent amenities, including a fully equipped kitchen and fast Wi-Fi.

Located in a quiet area close to downtown, it provides easy access to public transit and major city attractions. The property is ideal for work trips and solo travelers seeking a peaceful stay. The neighborhood offers convenient access to markets and parks, with most of Toronto's popular sites within walking distance. The guest house is not a party hostel, making it suitable for those preferring a quieter environment.

Nearby Attractions: Within walking distance to Nathan Phillips Square, Yonge/Dundas Square, and various other attractions.

TRAVEL

DATE:

DURATION:

DESTINATION:

PLACES TO SEE:

1 _____
2 _____
3 _____
4 _____
5 _____
6 _____
7 _____

LOCAL FOOD TO TRY:

1 _____
2 _____
3 _____
4 _____
5 _____
6 _____
7 _____

NOTES

EXPENSES IN TOTAL:

JOURNAL

RESTAURANT

SOCO Kitchen + Bar

Location: 75 Lower Simcoe St, Toronto, ON M5J 3A6, Canada

Plus code: JJV8+5F Toronto, Ontario, Canada

Contact: +1 416-637-5465

Website: www.socokitchenandbar.ca

Opening hours: Monday to Sunday: 7am – 11pm

Description: SOCO Kitchen + Bar is located within the Delta Hotels Toronto, offering a vibrant dining experience with a rooftop bar. The restaurant features a diverse menu with a focus on comfort food and hearty dishes suitable for various tastes. The ambiance is casual yet sophisticated, making it a great spot for both business meals and social gatherings. The rooftop bar provides a pleasant setting with city views, ideal for enjoying cocktails or light bites. The establishment offers a range of dishes including salads, burgers, and specialty items. The price range for meals is approximately $20–$40 per person. Notable offerings include their curry dishes and a variety of vegetarian options. It's worth noting that gluten-free options are limited, so diners with dietary restrictions may need to consider alternatives.

Nearby Attractions: The restaurant is situated in downtown Toronto, close to attractions such as the Ripley's Aquarium of Canada and the CN Tower, making it a convenient dining option for those exploring the area.

Insomnia Restaurant and Lounge

Location: 563 Bloor St W, Toronto, ON M5S 1Y6, Canada

Plus code: MH8Q+2M Toronto, Ontario, Canada

Contact: +1 416-588-3907

Website: www.insomniarestaurant.com
Opening hours: Monday to Sunday: 11am – 2am
Description: Insomnia Restaurant and Lounge is a vibrant dining spot located on Bloor Street West. The restaurant offers a diverse menu with a focus on brunch and dinner options, featuring dishes like omelettes, waffles, chicken, tacos, and burgers. Known for its cozy and stylish interior, Insomnia provides a welcoming atmosphere for both casual dining and social gatherings. Meals are priced between $20 and $70 per person, depending on the order. The restaurant is popular for its hearty portions and friendly service, with brunch items including a standout steak and eggs. Insomnia is LGBTQ+ friendly and also offers a selection of cocktails and desserts. It's a great choice for those looking to enjoy a late-night meal or a relaxed brunch in a lively setting.
Nearby Attractions: Located in the vibrant Bloorcourt neighborhood, the restaurant is close to attractions such as the Royal Ontario Museum and the University of Toronto, making it a convenient stop for those exploring the area.

Rodney's Oyster House
Location: 469 King St W, Toronto, ON M5V 1K4, Canada
Plus code: MH8Q+2M Toronto, Ontario, Canada
Contact: +1 416-504-6262
Website: www.rodneysoysterhouse.com
Opening hours: Friday to Saturday: 12pm – 12am Sunday to Thursday: 12pm – 10pm
Description: Rodney's Oyster House is a renowned seafood establishment located on King Street West, celebrated for its fresh oysters and seafood dishes. The restaurant offers a range of seafood options, including crab cakes, clams, and lobster, in a charming and vibrant setting. Known for its extensive selection of oysters and handcrafted sauces, Rodney's provides a delightful dining experience for seafood enthusiasts. The atmosphere is lively, making it an excellent choice for both casual meals and special occasions. The price range for a meal typically falls between $40 and $100 per person. The restaurant is also noted for its knowledgeable staff and excellent service. Guests should be aware that some dishes may use alcohol

in the cooking process, so it's advisable to inform the staff of any dietary restrictions related to alcohol.

Nearby Attractions: Situated in the lively King Street West area, Rodney's Oyster House is close to attractions such as the TIFF Bell Lightbox and the Entertainment District, making it a convenient dining spot for those exploring the neighborhood.

Wilbur Mexicana

Location: 552 King St W, Toronto, ON M5V 1M3, Canada
Plus code: JJV2+XF Toronto, Ontario, Canada
Opening hours: Monday to Sunday: 11am – 10pm
Description: Wilbur Mexicana is a popular Mexican restaurant located on King Street West, offering a vibrant and casual dining experience. Known for its delicious tacos and extensive salsa bar, the restaurant provides a variety of fresh, flavorful options including street corn and nachos. Customers can choose from a range of salsas, from mild to extremely spicy, to complement their meals. The establishment features a take-away and fast-casual atmosphere, with friendly staff and prompt service. The price range for a meal is typically between $10 and $40 per person, depending on the order. The restaurant is an excellent choice for those seeking high-quality Mexican food in a lively setting.

Nearby Attractions: Wilbur Mexicana is situated in the lively King Street West area, close to attractions such as the TIFF Bell Lightbox and the Entertainment District, making it a convenient dining option for those exploring the neighborhood.

Valens Restaurant Inc
Location: 19 Baldwin St, Toronto, ON M5T 1L1, Canada
Plus code: MJ44+CR Toronto, Ontario, Canada
Contact: +1 416-340-0303
Website: valens.ca

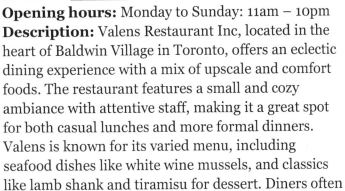

Opening hours: Monday to Sunday: 11am – 10pm
Description: Valens Restaurant Inc, located in the heart of Baldwin Village in Toronto, offers an eclectic dining experience with a mix of upscale and comfort foods. The restaurant features a small and cozy ambiance with attentive staff, making it a great spot for both casual lunches and more formal dinners. Valens is known for its varied menu, including seafood dishes like white wine mussels, and classics like lamb shank and tiramisu for dessert. Diners often enjoy fixed-price menus, such as those offered during Toronto's Summerlicious event, which are affordable yet flavorful. Although portions can be on the smaller side, the taste and quality of the food remain highly praised. The restaurant's atmosphere is intimate but can get busy, so reservations are recommended. Prices range from $20 to $40 per person, depending on the meal.
Nearby Attractions: Valens is located in Baldwin Village, a charming area known for its mix of restaurants and shops. Nearby, you can explore the Art Gallery of Ontario, the University of Toronto, and Kensington Market, making it an ideal location for dining after a day of exploring Toronto's cultural and historic landmarks.

La Vecchia Restaurant Uptown
Location: 2405 Yonge St A, Toronto, ON M4P 2E7, Canada
Plus code: PJ62+3F Toronto, Ontario, Canada

Contact: +1 416-489-0630

Website: lavecchia.ca

Opening hours:
- Friday: 11:30 am–11 pm
- Saturday: 11 am–11 pm
- Sunday: 10 am–10:30 pm
- Monday to Thursday: 11:30 am–10:30 pm

Description: La Vecchia Restaurant Uptown offers an authentic Italian dining experience in Toronto's Yonge Street neighborhood. The restaurant boasts a cozy yet elegant ambiance with attentive service that elevates the dining experience. With a diverse menu featuring Italian classics like rigatoni, pizza, and seafood specials, the dishes are praised for their flavorful execution, though some may feel portions are on the smaller side for the price. Notable dishes include the Gioia pizza with a honey drizzle and jalapeños, rigatoni Romani, and specials like halibut with lemon risotto and braised short ribs.

While the food quality and atmosphere often receive high praise, the consistency in portions and temperature of dishes can vary. Still, patrons appreciate the well-crafted Italian dishes, large dessert portions, and strong coffee. La Vecchia also offers an inviting dining space for both casual meals and special occasions, making it a popular spot for lovers of Italian cuisine.

Nearby Attractions:

Located in a bustling part of Yonge Street, La Vecchia Restaurant Uptown is situated near retail shops, theaters, and parks. It's an ideal spot for a pre- or post-event meal or simply to enjoy a leisurely lunch or dinner in a vibrant part of Toronto.

Valens Restaurant Inc
Location: 19 Baldwin St, Toronto, ON M5T 1L1, Canada
Plus code: MJ44+CR Toronto, Ontario, Canada
Contact: +1 416-340-0303
Website: valens.ca

Opening hours:
- Friday to Sunday: 11 am–10 pm
- Monday to Thursday: 11 am–10 pm

Description:

Valens Restaurant, located in the Baldwin Village of Toronto, offers a casual dining experience with a menu that caters to various palates, featuring comfort classics and European-inspired dishes. It's particularly popular during the city's Summerlicious event, offering prix-fixe menus at competitive prices. The atmosphere is intimate but small, which may lead to delays in service during busier hours.

The food is well-regarded for its flavors, with standout dishes such as the white wine mussels, braised lamb shank, and decadent crème brûlée. However, some patrons mention smaller entrée portions and occasional inconsistencies with the temperature of dishes. On the other hand, dessert portions tend to be large and satisfying.

While service is generally attentive, some diners have noted issues with reservations and seating, especially during peak times. Overall, Valens is a solid choice for those looking for a satisfying meal in the Baldwin Village area, with well-prepared food and a warm atmosphere.

Nearby Attractions:

Baldwin Village is known for its eclectic mix of restaurants, boutique shops, and nearby cultural spots like the Art Gallery of Ontario and Kensington Market, making Valens a convenient stop for a meal while exploring the area.

Scaddabush Italian Kitchen & Bar - Front Street

Location: 200 Front St W, Unit #G001, Toronto, ON M5V 3J1, Canada Located at Simcoe Place

Plus code: JJV7+WR Toronto, Ontario, Canada

Contact: +1 416-979-3665

Website: scaddabush.com

Opening hours:

- Monday to Sunday: 11:30 am–12 am

Description: Scaddabush Italian Kitchen & Bar is a casual yet trendy Italian restaurant chain known for its lively ambiance and rustic, cozy decor featuring wooden elements and wine displays. Situated in the heart of Toronto near major attractions like Rogers Centre, it's a great option for those attending concerts or events. The restaurant offers a variety of Italian-inspired dishes ranging from appetizers like fried spaghetti balls and spinach artichoke dip to main courses including pizza, gnocchi, and classic pastas.

The service is generally attentive, with friendly staff and a welcoming atmosphere. Diners recommend the Caesar salad and tiramisu, with positive feedback on the flavorful and well-cooked pizzas. However, some have experienced inconsistency in the quality of pasta dishes. Despite occasional slower service during busy periods, the lively atmosphere and delicious dishes make Scaddabush a popular spot for both lunch and dinner.

Menu highlights:
- Fried Spaghetti Balls
- Caesar Salad
- Spinach and Artichoke Dip
- Straight Up Meatball
- Tiramisu
- Gnocchi
- Variety of pizzas

Atmosphere:
The restaurant features warm lighting, leather seats, and a mixture of wooden and wine-themed decor. The vibe is energetic and welcoming, making it great for both casual get-togethers and family meals. Scaddabush also offers a patio for outdoor dining, which is especially pleasant during warm weather.

Nearby Attractions:
Scaddabush is conveniently located near major Toronto landmarks such as the Rogers Centre, making it an ideal stop before or after events, concerts, and sports games.

Parking:
Nearby parking is available for a fee.

Price range:
- Apps & small plates: $10–$20
- Mains & pastas: $30–$50
- Price per person: ~$40–$100 depending on meal choice and drinks

Sunrise Tree Guest House

Location: 15 Chapman Ave, Toronto, ON M4B 1C3, Canada

Plus code: PM2X+2C Toronto, Ontario, Canada

Contact: +1 647-687-7148

Website: sunrisetreebnb.ca

Check-in time: 5:00 PM

Check-out time: 1:00 PM

Overview: Sunrise Tree Guest House is a small bed and breakfast in Toronto, offering a warm and cozy atmosphere. The host, Dinh, is known for fast communication and attention to detail. The property is accessible by car or public transport, and parking is available on the street. Guests have described the rooms as clean, comfortable, and quiet.

Sunrise Tree Guest House has received mixed feedback. While many guests have enjoyed their stays, describing the property as clean and welcoming, a few issues related to advertising accuracy and reports of bugs have been raised. The host has disputed the bug claim and stands by the cleanliness of the guest house.

TRAVEL

DATE:

DURATION:

DESTINATION:

PLACES TO SEE:

1
2
3
4
5
6
7

LOCAL FOOD TO TRY:

1
2
3
4
5
6
7

NOTES

EXPENSES IN TOTAL:

JOURNAL

Royal Canadian Gifts

Location: 229 Spadina Ave., Toronto, ON M5T 2E2, Canada
Plus Code: MJ23+G5 Toronto, Ontario, Canada
Contact: +1 416-598-1988
Website: www.ucanada.com
Open Time:
Friday: 10 am–8 pm
Saturday: 11 am–7:30 pm
Sunday: 11 am–7:30 pm
Monday: 10 am–8 pm
Tuesday: 10 am–8 pm
Wednesday: 10 am–8 pm
Thursday: 10 am–8 pm

Description: Royal Canadian Gifts, located in downtown Toronto at 229 Spadina Ave., offers a vast selection of Canadian-themed merchandise perfect for tourists and locals alike. Known for its high-quality products compared to other shops in the Chinatown area, this store provides a comprehensive range of souvenirs, including keychains, shirts, clocks, and Canadian snacks. Visitors can find authentic Jakeman's maple syrup, unavailable in neighboring stores, alongside a wide variety of other items like pins, apparel, and Canadian candies. Whether you're looking for affordable trinkets or higher-end mementos, Royal Canadian Gifts caters to all budgets with well-organized displays in a clean, well-maintained environment. Open daily, this shop is a top destination for those wanting to bring a piece of Canada home.

A & F Canada Gifts

Location: 273 Spadina Ave., Toronto, ON M5T 2E3, Canada
Plus Code: MJ32+3W Toronto, Ontario, Canada
Contact: +1 416-348-9674

Website: www.anfcanadagifts.ca
Open Time: 11 am–7 pm
Description: A & F Canada Gifts, located at 273 Spadina Ave., Toronto, is a family-run business with over 20 years of experience offering a wide selection of Canadian souvenirs. Situated in the heart of Chinatown, this shop is well-known for its affordable prices, quality merchandise, and friendly customer service. Visitors can find a diverse range of items, including keychains, mugs, clothes, maple syrup bottles, and cookies, all displayed in a well-organized environment. In addition to traditional souvenirs, the store carries Toronto sports team caps and toques, as well as some local art. The quality of their Canada-branded shirts makes them versatile for daily wear, while the welcoming atmosphere adds to the charm of shopping here. Whether you're short on time or looking for a comprehensive selection, A & F Canada Gifts ensures a great shopping experience in downtown Toronto.

Toronto Best Souvenirs
Location: 145 Queens Quay W, Toronto, ON M5J 2H4, Canada
Plus Code: JJQ9+VX Toronto, Ontario, Canada
Contact: +1 647-885-3118
Website: www.torontosbestsouvenirs.com
Open Time: 11 am–6 pm
Description: Located at 145 Queens Quay W, Toronto Best Souvenirs provides a selection of souvenirs and gifts suitable for visitors looking for mementos of their time in Toronto. The store offers various items, although it may not have the most extensive collection compared to other souvenir shops in the area. Open daily, it provides a convenient option for those exploring the waterfront area. The store's staff are known for being friendly, and the environment is clean and welcoming. Despite occasional concerns about inconsistent opening hours and limited selection, it remains a practical stop for tourists looking to purchase souvenirs.

U Canada Gifts

Location: 302 Spadina Ave. Unit G102, Toronto, ON M5T 2E7, Canada

Plus Code: MJ32+8H Toronto, Ontario, Canada

Contact: +1 416-977-5888

Website: www.ucanada.com

Open Time: 11 am–8 pm

Description: U Canada Gifts, located in the W & H.S Commercial Building at 302 Spadina Ave., offers a diverse range of Canadian-themed souvenirs and gifts. The store features a spacious and pleasant atmosphere, making it easy to browse through their selection of items. Visitors can find a variety of products including creative magnets, cups, clothes, hats, badges, dolls, and maple syrup. The store also offers unique items such as small soju cups and international postcards. Although prices may be higher compared to other stores, the quality and variety of merchandise, along with friendly staff, contribute to a positive shopping experience. Whether you're looking for something special to remember your trip or a unique gift, U Canada Gifts provides a well-rounded selection.

Famous Canada Inc

Location: 222 Spadina Ave. #105, Toronto, ON M5T 2C2, Canada

Plus Code: MJ22+9X Toronto, Ontario, Canada

Contact: +1 416-979-7988

Open Time: 10 am–7 pm

Description: Located at 222 Spadina Ave. in the Chinatown Centre, Famous Canada Inc offers a wide variety of Canadian souvenirs at affordable prices. The store is known for its clean and bright environment, making it a pleasant place to shop. It features a range of items including T-shirts, caps, shorts, and pants, catering to both adults and children. The store is appreciated for its friendly staff and extensive selection, making it a popular choice for those looking to purchase souvenirs before heading abroad. While it is a well-regarded destination for souvenirs, be aware that the store prefers cash payments and prices may be higher due to inflation.

St Lawrence Smoke & Gift Shop
Location: 93 Front St E, Toronto, ON M5E 1C3, Canada
Plus Code: JJXH+J7 Toronto, Ontario, Canada
Contact: +1 416-363-8252
Open Time: 9 am–7 pm
Saturday: 7 am–5 pm
Sunday: 10 am–5 pm
Monday: Closed

Description: Located within St. Lawrence Market at 93 Front St E, St Lawrence Smoke & Gift Shop offers a range of Toronto and Canadian souvenirs. This shop features an assortment of items including keyrings, doll magnets, and other keepsakes, known for their variety and reasonable prices. The store is appreciated for its friendly atmosphere and is run by a welcoming owner, providing a personal touch to the shopping experience. It is a convenient spot for finding well-priced souvenirs with a good selection, making it a recommended stop for visitors exploring the market.

Blue Banana Market
Location: 250 Augusta Ave, Toronto, ON M5T 2L7, Canada
Plus Code: MH4W+7W Toronto, Ontario, Canada
Contact: +1 416-594-6600
Website: www.bbmgifts.com
Open Time: 11 am–7 pm

Description: Blue Banana Market, situated at 250 Augusta Ave in Kensington Market, is a vibrant shop known for its eclectic assortment of gifts, souvenirs, and home decor. This LGBTQ+ friendly store features a broad selection of items including novelty socks, trinkets, kitchen decor, and a variety of unique candies and hot sauces, some of which are featured in the Hot Ones interviews. The market is well-regarded for its diverse range of products and price points, making it an ideal destination for finding quirky and fun gifts for all ages. Though the washrooms are located on a different floor and may require a code, the store's friendly staff and wide-ranging inventory contribute to a distinctive shopping experience.

Better Gift Shop
Location: 558 Dundas St W, Toronto, ON M5T 1H3, Canada
Plus Code: MJ32+34 Toronto, Ontario, Canada
Contact: +1 416-979-2345
Website: www.bettergiftshop.com
Open Time: 12–7 pm
Sunday: 12–5 pm
Monday: 12–6 pm
Tuesday: 12–6 pm
Description: Better Gift Shop, located at 558 Dundas St W, offers a unique shopping experience with a focus on distinctive and stylish gifts and personal items. The store features a curated selection of streetwear essentials from popular brands such as Cav Empt, Arc'teryx, Salomon, Full Court Press, and Gramicci, alongside a range of trinkets and home goods. Known for its high-profile collaborations and limited edition products, the shop attracts fashion enthusiasts and collectors. The friendly and knowledgeable staff provide helpful advice and recommendations, enhancing the shopping experience. Better Gift Shop is celebrated for its unique merchandise and exceptional service, making it a noteworthy destination for discovering exclusive items in Toronto.

Lucky's Trading Co. Ltd.

Location: 427 Spadina Ave., Toronto, ON M5T 2G6, Canada

Plus Code: MJ42+V6 Toronto, Ontario, Canada

Description: Located at 427 Spadina Ave., Lucky's Trading Co. Ltd. offers a wide range of souvenirs at great value. The shop is known for its affordability and diverse selection of items, including unique artsy tea cups and other keepsakes. It provides a budget-friendly option for visitors looking for souvenirs in the area. The friendly service adds to the positive shopping experience, making it a notable stop for those seeking good deals and a variety of souvenirs.

3-Day Family Itinerary in Toronto

Day 1: Arrival and City Exploration

- **Morning:** Arrive at Toronto Pearson International Airport (YYZ).
- **Afternoon:** Check into your hotel and take a leisurely stroll through the Distillery District.
- **Evening:** Enjoy a family-friendly dinner at a local restaurant.

Day 2: Parks and Entertainment

- **Morning:** Visit High Park and enjoy a picnic or explore the zoo. [Free for park, approximately CAD$30-40 for zoo admission]
- **Afternoon:** Head to the Toronto Islands for a day of fun in the sun. [Varies depending on ferry fare]
- **Evening:** Catch a baseball game at the Rogers Centre. [Varies depending on ticket prices]

Day 3: Museums and Attractions

- **Morning:** Visit the Royal Ontario Museum to learn about Canada's history and culture. [Approximately CAD$20-30 for admission]
- **Afternoon:** Explore the Ontario Science Centre for interactive exhibits and hands-on fun. [Approximately CAD$30-40 for admission]
- **Evening:** Enjoy a family-friendly dinner at a local restaurant. [Varies depending on the restaurant]

Additional Activities:

- **Ripley's Aquarium of Canada:** Explore the underwater world and encounter diverse marine life. [Approximately CAD$30-40 for admission]
- **Hockey Hall of Fame:** Learn about Canada's national sport and see the Stanley Cup. [Approximately CAD$20-30 for admission]

- **Toronto Police Museum and Discovery Centre:** Discover the history of policing in Toronto. [Approximately CAD$10-15 for admission]

- **Spadina Museum:** Step back in time and explore a historic Victorian mansion. [Approximately CAD$10-15 for admission]

- **St. Lawrence Market:** Sample fresh produce, meats, and artisanal goods.

- **The Distillery District:** Explore this historic neighborhood turned arts and entertainment hub.

7-DAY ROMANTIC GETAWAY IN TORONTO FOR COUPLES

Day 1: Arrival and Relaxation

- **Morning:** Arrive at Toronto Pearson International Airport (YYZ).

- **Afternoon:** Take a taxi or public transportation to your hotel. [Approximately CAD$50-70 for a taxi]

- **Evening:** Indulge in a romantic dinner at a waterfront restaurant. [Varies depending on the restaurant]

Day 2: Historic Charm

- **Morning:** Visit Casa Loma and explore its beautiful gardens. [Approximately CAD$20-30 for admission]

- **Afternoon:** Take a leisurely walk through High Park and enjoy a picnic.

- **Evening:** Attend a romantic dinner theater performance at the Pantages Theatre.

Day 3: Niagara Falls Day Trip

- **Morning:** Take a day trip to Niagara Falls by bus or train. [Approximately CAD$50-70 for transportation, additional costs for activities]

- **Afternoon:** Enjoy a romantic boat tour or a wine tasting in the nearby Niagara-on-the-Lake region. [Varies depending on tours and tastings]

Day 4: Island Escape

- **Morning:** Take a ferry to the Toronto Islands and rent bicycles for a romantic ride. [Varies depending on ferry fare and bike rentals]
- **Afternoon:** Relax on the beach and enjoy a picnic lunch.
- **Evening:** Enjoy a romantic dinner cruise on Lake Ontario. [Varies depending on the cruise]

Day 5: Cultural Exploration

- **Morning:** Visit the Art Gallery of Ontario to admire world-class art collections. [Approximately CAD$20-30 for admission]
- **Afternoon:** Explore the vibrant Kensington Market and sample international cuisine.
- **Evening:** Attend a jazz concert at a local venue. [Varies depending on the venue and performance]

Day 6: Waterfront Relaxation

- **Morning:** Stroll along the Harbourfront Centre and enjoy the waterfront views.
- **Afternoon:** Take a boat tour of the Toronto Harbour and admire the city skyline.
- **Evening:** Indulge in a romantic dinner at a waterfront restaurant.

Day 7: Departure

- **Morning:** Check out of your hotel and head to the airport for your flight home.

Additional Romantic Activities:

- **Hot Air Balloon Ride:** Enjoy breathtaking panoramic views of Toronto. [Varies depending on the company]
- **Spa Day:** Relax and rejuvenate at a luxury spa. [Varies depending on the spa and treatments]

- **Horse-Drawn Carriage Ride:** Take a romantic ride through the city. [Varies depending on the company]
- **Stargazing:** Enjoy a romantic evening under the stars.

10-DAY TORONTO ITINERARY

Day 1: Arrival and Orientation

- **Morning:** Arrive at Toronto Pearson International Airport (YYZ).
- **Afternoon:** Take a taxi or public transportation to your hotel. [Approximately CAD$50-70 for a taxi]
- **Evening:** Explore the CN Tower for panoramic views of the city. [Approximately CAD$40-60 for admission]

Day 2: Historic Toronto

- **Morning:** Visit the Royal Ontario Museum to learn about Canada's history and culture. [Approximately CAD$20-30 for admission]
- **Afternoon:** Explore Fort York National Historic Site and discover the city's military past.
- **Evening:** Enjoy a performance at the Aga Khan Museum.

Day 3: Nature and Wildlife

- **Morning:** Hike through High Park and visit the Toronto Zoo. [Free for High Park, approximately CAD$30-40 for zoo admission]
- **Afternoon:** Relax on the Toronto Islands and enjoy the beach.
- **Evening:** Catch a baseball game at the Rogers Centre.

Day 4: Cultural Exploration

- **Morning:** Visit the Art Gallery of Ontario to admire world-class art collections. [Approximately CAD$20-30 for admission]

- **Afternoon:** Explore the vibrant Kensington Market and sample international cuisine.
- **Evening:** Enjoy a live performance at the Pantages Theatre.

Day 5: Niagara Falls Day Trip

- **Morning:** Take a day trip to Niagara Falls by bus or train. [Approximately CAD$50-70 for transportation, additional costs for activities]
- **Afternoon:** Explore the Niagara-on-the-Lake wine region and enjoy a wine tasting.

Day 6: Parks and Gardens

- **Morning:** Visit Casa Loma and explore its beautiful gardens. [Approximately CAD$20-30 for admission]
- **Afternoon:** Relax in Trinity Bellwoods Park and enjoy a picnic.
- **Evening:** Catch a movie at the TIFF Bell Lightbox. [Approximately CAD$15-20 for tickets]

Day 7: Waterfront and Islands

- **Morning:** Explore the Harbourfront Centre and enjoy the waterfront views.
- **Afternoon:** Take a ferry to the Toronto Islands and visit Centreville Amusement Park. [Varies depending on ferry fare and amusement park tickets]
- **Evening:** Dine at a waterfront restaurant and enjoy the sunset. [Varies depending on the restaurant]

Day 8: Museums and Attractions

- **Morning:** Visit the Hockey Hall of Fame and learn about Canada's national sport. [Approximately CAD$20-30 for admission]
- **Afternoon:** Explore the Toronto Police Museum and Discovery Centre. [Approximately CAD$10-15 for admission]
- **Evening:** Enjoy a comedy show at the Second City Theatre. [Varies depending on the show]

Day 9: Local Neighborhoods

- **Morning:** Explore the Annex neighborhood and visit the Spadina Museum. [Approximately CAD$10-15 for admission]

- **Afternoon:** Stroll through the Village of Yorkville and shop at luxury boutiques.

- **Evening:** Enjoy a dinner cruise on Lake Ontario. [Varies depending on the cruise]

Day 10: Departure

- **Morning:** Check out of your hotel and head to the airport for your flight home.

Note: These are approximate costs and may vary depending on your choices and the time of year. Be sure to research specific attractions and transportation options for the most accurate pricing.

DID YOU KNOW?

1. **Did You Know?** Toronto is home to the CN Tower, once the world's tallest freestanding structure, standing at 1,815 feet.
2. **Did You Know?** Toronto is one of the most multicultural cities in the world, with over 140 languages spoken.
3. **Did You Know?** The Toronto Islands, a popular recreational destination, are the largest car-free urban community in North America.
4. **Did You Know?** Toronto's PATH is the world's largest underground shopping complex, stretching over 30 kilometers.
5. **Did You Know?** Toronto is nicknamed "The 6ix," a term popularized by rapper Drake, who is originally from the city.
6. **Did You Know?** The Royal Ontario Museum houses over 6 million objects and is one of the largest museums in North America.
7. **Did You Know?** Toronto has a castle! Casa Loma, built in 1914, is a Gothic Revival-style mansion that's now a popular tourist attraction.
8. **Did You Know?** Toronto hosts the Toronto International Film Festival (TIFF), one of the most prestigious film festivals in the world.
9. **Did You Know?** The Toronto Zoo is one of the largest in the world, with over 5,000 animals representing more than 500 species.
10. **Did You Know?** Toronto was originally named "York" when it was founded in 1793 and was later renamed in 1834.
11. **Did You Know?** The Toronto Maple Leafs, one of the NHL's most famous teams, has a passionate fan base despite not winning the Stanley Cup since 1967.
12. **Did You Know?** Toronto's Distillery District is the largest collection of Victorian-era industrial architecture in North America.
13. **Did You Know?** The Toronto Raptors are the only Canadian team in the NBA and won their first championship in 2019.
14. **Did You Know?** Toronto's Eaton Centre is one of the busiest shopping malls in North America, attracting over 50 million visitors annually.
15. **Did You Know?** The Toronto Islands were formed by a series of storms in the mid-19th century, separating them from the mainland.
16. **Did You Know?** Toronto is often used as a stand-in for New York City in movies and TV shows due to its similar skyline.

17. **Did You Know?** The Gooderham Building, known as the Flatiron Building, predates New York City's more famous Flatiron Building by ten years.
18. **Did You Know?** Toronto's St. Lawrence Market has been named one of the best food markets in the world by National Geographic.
19. **Did You Know?** The Toronto International Film Festival's People's Choice Award is often a predictor of future Oscar winners.
20. **Did You Know?** The city of Toronto has over 1,500 parks and 600 kilometers of trails, offering endless opportunities for outdoor activities.

Made in the USA
Middletown, DE
29 April 2025

74911523R00090